Osprey Modelling • 2

M000304859

Modelling the Messerschmitt Bf 110

Brett Green

Consultant editor Robert Oehler
Series editors Marcus Cowper and Nikolai Bogdanovic ·

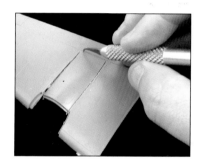

First published in Great Britain in 2003 by Osprey Publishing, Elms Court,
Chapel Way, Botley, Oxford OX2 9LP, United Kingdom.
Email: info@ospreypublishing.com

ISBN 1 84176 704 2

Editorial by Ilios Publishing, Oxford, UK (www.iliospublishing.com)
Design: Servis Filmsetting Ltd, Manchester, UK
Index by Alison Worthington
Originated by Global Graphics, Czech Republic
Printed and bound by L-Rex Printing Company Ltd

03 04 05 06 07   10 9 8 7 6 5 4 3 2 1

A CIP catalogue record for this book is available from the British Library.

FOR A CATALOGUE OF ALL BOOKS PUBLISHED BY OSPREY MODELLING,
MILITARY AND AVIATION PLEASE CONTACT:

Osprey Direct UK, P.O. Box 140, Wellingborough,
Northants, NN8 2FA, UK
E-mail: info@ospreydirect.co.uk

Osprey Direct USA, c/o MBI Publishing, P.O. Box 1,
729 Prospect Ave, Osceola, WI 54020, USA
E-mail: info@ospreydirectusa.com

www.ospreypublishing.com

Acknowledgments

It has been my pleasure and privilege to work with Chris
Wauchop on several of the models seen in the following pages.
Chris's results are superb, and this book benefits greatly from his
talent and insights.

Dr Charles Metz has also been a great help in confirming the
actual shape of the Messerschmitt Bf 110G engine cowling and
by supplying the comprehensive Bf 110 reading list at the end
of this book. He was also instrumental in helping identify the
characteristics of Bf 110 variants, both directly and via the
excellent research pieces on the subject by himself and George
Hopp. Thanks to Steven Eisenman for pointing me in the
direction of the Metz/Hopp Bf 110 articles in the first place.

Chris Kowall also kindly sent me his accurate drawings of the
Messerschmitt Bf 110F/G cowling.

I am grateful to Scotty Battistoni and Dave Klaus at Meteor
Productions, who answered my pleas for a 1/48-scale
Messerschmitt Bf 110F/G Correction Set. Scotty did a superb job
in designing and producing this resin set.

And, as always, when I am in the basement building, painting,
photographing or writing, my wife Debbie is upstairs shouldering
the extra burden. Thank you, Debbie, for making this book
possible.

Contents

The Messerschmitt Bf 110 in World War II

The Messerschmitt Bf 110 was undoubtedly one of the most significant aircraft of World War II, yet it was branded a failure as early as the end of the Battle of Britain.

In those summer months of 1940, Messerschmitt Bf 110s on long-range escort missions suffered heavy losses to Spitfires and Hurricanes. Eventually, Messerschmitt Bf 110s had to be escorted themselves by the more nimble Bf 109s.

The Battle of Britain proved that the Messerschmitt Bf 110 was no match for an agile single-engine fighter in a dogfight. However, the fact that this shortcoming was not foreseen prior to the Battle of Britain was not the fault of the Bf 110. Luftwaffe tacticians should have anticipated the consequences of pitting the slower and less manoeuvrable Bf 110 against modern British fighters, especially after first-hand encounters in the previous months over the skies of France.

Despite these setbacks in the summer of 1940, the Messerschmitt Bf 110 continued to be used effectively in other theatres and roles until the last days of the War.

It served on the Eastern Front in large numbers. Bf 110 units made a significant contribution to destroying the Soviet Air Force on the ground in the opening days of Operation Barbarossa. As the nature of the campaign in the East changed, the Bf 110 was instrumental in the destruction of thousands of Soviet vehicles, including tanks.

In North Africa, a single Bf 110 *Gruppe* performed the roles of heavy fighter, bomber and ground attack. III.ZG 26 (the third *Gruppe* of the 26th *Zerstörergruppe*) had considerable success despite the demanding workload and allied air superiority

The Bf 110 also made its presence felt during the campaign in Crete, in the war on Allied shipping in the Arctic and, later, through its sacrificial role in defence of Germany against daylight bombers.

The concept of a twin-engine heavy fighter was pursued in the 1930s by a number of European nations including France, Poland, Britain and Germany. The

Fujimi's old but generally accurate 1/48-scale Messerschmitt Bf 110C/D kit, depicted as a Bf 110D from ZG 26 in flight over the Mediterranean during 1941.

theory was that a powerful, heavily armed, long-range aircraft could perform a number of roles, including bomber escort, troop support, heavy fighter and light bomber. France developed the Potez 63 for these tasks; Poland's version was the PZL P.38; and Great Britain had the Westland Whirlwind.

The Luftwaffe selected the Messerschmitt Bf 110 as their preferred *Zerstörer* (Destroyer) aircraft ahead of competitors from Focke-Wulf and Henschel. The Daimler Benz DB601 engine was eventually approved as the power plant for the production version of the Bf 110. Manufacturing delays meant that the first 45 airframes were completed as the Messerschmitt Bf 110B, equipped with the 470 kW Junkers Jumo 210Da engine. The first definitive version fitted with DB601 engine, the Messerschmitt Bf 110C, began production in early 1939. By September 1939, 159 Messerschmitt Bf 110Cs were available to the Luftwaffe.

The Messerschmitt Bf 110 entered World War II as a new and prestigious weapon for the Luftwaffe, performing bomber escort, heavy fighter and troop support roles during the German invasion of Poland. It performed well against Polish fighters and put its heavy armament to effective use against ground targets

Early versions of the Bf 110 served as night fighters without the aid of radar. In common with most German night fighters of the period, this Messerschmitt Bf 110E is painted overall black.

after the Luftwaffe had established air superiority. The Bf 110 repeated these roles during the campaign in the West, where its long range was especially useful for escorting bombers deep into France. The twin-engine Messerschmitt was more than a match for most contemporary French fighters, but early encounters with Spitfires and Hurricanes resulted in unaccustomedly heavy losses. This was an ominous indicator of the coming months over the British Isles.

Even if its fortunes as a pure fighter aircraft were mixed, the Messerschmitt Bf 110 had a better record as a defensive weapon.

As early as December 1939, Bf 110C aircraft of I./ZG 76 were involved in the decimation of an armed reconnaissance patrol over the Heligoland Bight. Eight Wellingtons out of a total 22 on patrol were claimed by the *Zerstörers*. This single event put massed daylight bombing off the British agenda until 1943, and ZG 2 and ZG 76 continued to enjoy superiority over the Blenheims and Wellingtons of the RAF in the following months.

Arguably the most important contribution made to the German war effort by the Messerschmitt Bf 110 was as a night fighter. The role was initially ad hoc. From July 1940, day fighters were simply painted black and sent aloft to deal with British bombers, which were now making their attacks under the relative protection of darkness. These early night fighters had no specialised equipment or ground control assistance. Enemy aircraft were held in the cone of a searchlight, and the Bf 110 would engage the bomber while it was illuminated in the beam.

This primitive tactic was soon replaced with a network of radar stations and ground stations. Personnel at the ground stations would radio the position of targets to the night fighter pilot, who would receive ongoing assistance to until the bombers were intercepted.

The Messerschmitt Bf 110 initially proved to be the most popular night fighter because it was faster and more manoeuvrable than its contemporaries, the Ju 88 and Do 17/217. It was also easily able to outpace and outclimb its

ProModeler's 1/48-scale Messerschmitt Bf 110G-4 night fighter, built almost straight from the box.

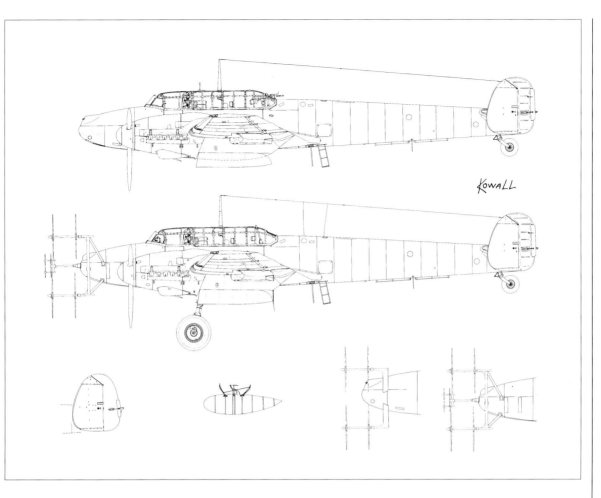

initial prey – the Wellington and the lumbering Whitley and Stirling bombers. However, changing tactics by Bomber Command and the inability to operate without visual confirmation of their targets demanded a new approach.

From February 1942, on-board radar was introduced to the Messerschmitt Bf 110. This coincided with the only major wartime redesign of the airframe, resulting in an interim type, the Bf 110F-4, and ultimately the Bf 110G-4. This variant remained the workhorse of the night fighter force from 1942 until the end of hostilities.

Identifying Messerschmitt Bf 110 variants

The Messerschmitt Bf 110 has presented some challenges to researchers trying to identify variants. The aircraft was in service and constant development through the war years with aerodynamic and power plant improvements, specialized versions, factory upgrades, field installation kits and local modifications all making positive identification of some aircraft difficult.

The table below is far from comprehensive, but it does provide some pointers for identifying variants by the style of the canopy, rudder, nose, pitot tube and other unique characteristics.

Please note that the table does not cover specialized variants (e.g. fighter/bomber, boat-tail, photo-reconnaissance etc.) nor tropical versions. Many Bf 110s also appeared as sub-types with specialized tropical equipment, bomb racks, reconnaissance cameras and/or life rafts in an extended tail. Further modifications were sometimes added in the field.

Messerschmitt Bf 110G-4 in 1/96 scale, original drawing by Chris Kowall. The top drawing depicts the standard fitout for the MG81Z machine gun in the rear cockpit; and a DF loop on the top of the canopy. The bottom drawing displays the upward firing twin Schrage Musik cannon (either MGFF/M 20mm or MK108 30mm) in the rear cockpit. The radar equipment on this aircraft is a combination of the FuG220 SN-2c 'antlers' and the smaller FuG212 on the nose. The smaller drawings at the bottom of the page show the smaller vertical tailplanes found on the Bf 110F-1/2 and Bf 110G-2 variants.

Characteristics of Bf 110 variants

Characteristic	Bf 110C	Bf 110D	Bf 110E	Bf 110F	BF 110G
Powerplant / Nacelles	DB601 early nacelles	DB601 or DB601N early nacelles	DB601N early nacelles (modified on E-3 Trop)	DB601F later style nacelles	DB605B later style nacelles
Variants	C-1 through 4 – heavy fighter boat-tail for stowage of dinghy (mid production onward) C-4/B – fighter/bomber C-5 – recon. C-5/N and C-7 DB601N engine	D-1 heavy fighter D-1/R1 – dachshund's belly 1,200l fuel tank D-2 – equipped for underwing drop tanks D-3 – Equipped with DB601N motor, fuel and oil drop tanks, and boat tail.	E-1 Fighter/Bomber E-2 – Boat Tail E-3 – Recon. /Trop – (may be applied to any variant). Tropicalised with dust filter on port-wing air intake and redesigned nacelle featuring deeper oil cooler housing	F-1 – fighter/bomber F-2 – heavy fighter (bomb racks removed) F-3 – recon. F-4 – night fighter	Field-installed weapon pack (Rüstsatz) capability across the range of 'G' variants G-2 – heavy fighter G-3 – recon. G-4 – night fighter
Typical Armament	4 x MG17 2 x MGFF 1 x MG17	4 x MG17 2 x MGFF 1 x MG17	4 x MG17 2 x MGFF 1 x MG17 ETC500/IXb bomb rack as standard equipment	4 x MG17 or 2 x MK 108 2 x MGFF or 2 x MG151/20 1 x MG17 or 1 x MG81Z	4 x MG17 or 2 x MK 108 2 x MG151/20 1 x MG81Z
Canopy Style	Early	Early	Early	Early or Late	Late
Rudder Style	Small	Small	Small	Small	Small or Large
Other external identifying characteristics		Armoured windscreen (indicative only)	Rectangular cooling vent on nose	Rectangular cooling vent on nose	Faired-in cooling vent on nose
Pitot Tube Location	Under wing	Under wing	Under wing	Under wing	Wing tip

Modelling the Messerschmitt Bf 110 in 1/48 scale

1/48-scale Messerschmitt Bf 110 kits

Brand	Description	Comments	Avail-ability	Stock No.
Fujimi	Messerschmitt Bf 110C/D	Generally good in outline with crisp surface features. Innacurate in several obvious areas. Sparse detail. Very poor interior.	Good	31002
Astrokit	Messerschmitt Bf 110C/D	Re-boxed Fujimi kit with Italian and German markings.	Limited	48103
Mauve	Messerschmitt Bf 110G-2	Based on the Fujimi kit with additional parts in high-quality injection-moulded plastic. Detail parts in white metal, photo-etched nickel and brass rod. Options of broad or narrow rudders, cannon or MG nose and canopy styles permits the depiction of either a Bf 110F or Bf 110G straight from the box.	Limited	ME00065
Revell	Messerschmitt Bf 110G-2	Actually depicts a Bf 110F. Very nice kit with high level of detail. Includes resin nose with machine gun armament and narrow rudders. Heavy day fighter version includes standard exhausts, W.Gr.50 rocket tubes and ventral cannon pack and resin nose. Poor depiction of engine nacelles.	Good	4164
Revell-Monogram	Messerschmitt Bf 110G-2	Same details as above but without the resin nose.	Good	5839
ProModeler	Messerschmitt Bf 110G-4	Very nice kit with high level of detail. Night fighter version with radar and flame damper exhausts. Poor depiction of engine nacelles.	Good	5933
Mauve	Messerschmitt Bf 110G-4	Based on the Fujimi kit with additional parts in high-quality injection-moulded plastic. Optional styles of radar included. Detail parts in white metal, photo-etched nickel and brass rod. Expensive.	Limited	ME00064

The Messerschmitt Bf 110 has not received as much attention in model form as its more glamorous stablemate, the Bf 109.

Even so, there are three very respectable mainstream kits available in 1/48 scale that permit the modeller to build most variants from the Bf 110C-1 to the ultimate Bf 110G-4. There is also a good selection of aftermarket detail sets, conversions, accessories and decals for day fighter and night fighter variants.

The Messerschmitt Bf 110 offers the modeller a fantastic range of colours, markings and variants, from the early-War green splinter schemes to the improvised markings of the Battle of Britain; grey *Zerstörers* adorned with garish bumblebee noses over the Steppes of Russia to yellow desert raiders; overall black night fighting pioneers to mottled hunters bristling with radar and guns.

The layout of the Messerschmitt Bf 110 is also ideal for modellers. In 1/48 scale, the Bf 110 is big enough to be impressive, but not too big to display. The long glasshouse canopy will reward the modeller who puts in the extra effort

to detail the interior. The cannon bay, engine compartments and large wheel wells almost beg for attention.

The modeller has the choice of three mainstream, injection-moulded Messerschmitt Bf 110 kits. The Fujimi kit covers early Bf 110C/D variants while the second choice is the ProModeler Messerschmitt Bf 110G-4 Night Fighter, released in 1997 by Revell-Monogram.

Finally, Revell-Monogram also offered a Messerschmitt Bf 110G-2 heavy day fighter with different tail surfaces, nose, exhausts, ordnance and pitot tube. Radar was not included with this version. This model was also offered with a different resin nose in the markings of ZG 1, the *Wespen Geschwader*.

Building Fujimi's Messerschmitt Bf 110C/D/E

Fujimi's Bf 110 in the box

Fujimi first released their 1/48-scale Messerschmitt Bf 110C around 1973 but re-released the model in 1987 with additional parts for a Bf 110D. The revised kit also included more stores and better decals. Although these kits are getting quite old, they are regularly re-released and frequently seen for sale both at model club meetings and on the Internet.

The 1987 version of the kit comprises 120 parts in grey plastic and 7 parts in clear plastic. The parts are well moulded with finely recessed panel lines. These later mouldings are showing signs of their age though, as some of the panel lines have almost disappeared from the nose and the bottom of the fuselage.

The overall shape of the model is pleasing and looks generally accurate. The rear fuselage seems a little slim, but this is not a serious issue.

One of the popular myths surrounding Fujimi's Bf 110 is that it is actually closer to 1/50 scale than 1/48 scale. This is not correct. In fact, the kit scales out to within one millimetre of published dimensions for overall length and wing span. Even the wing chord (width of the wing), which has also been called into question, is almost exactly in line with the published dimensions at the wing root (the area where the fuselage meets the wing).

The kit includes a number of extras including the dachshund belly 1,200l fuel tank, bombs, 300l drop tanks, 900l drop tanks, oil drop tank and boat tail. Optional position canopies are also supplied – a single-piece forward section with the canopy closed or four clear pieces comprising the windscreen with separate top flap and side windows.

On the other hand, the kit does suffer from some shortcomings. The interior is very poor. Fictional sidewall detail and an inaccurate, solid cockpit floor are combined with two bad seats and a decal instrument panel. The rear machine gun pivots on an overscale plastic post. Wheel well detail is entirely non-existent.

The exterior of the aircraft also betrays the model's vintage in a few areas. The accuracy of the ETC 500/IXb bomb rack under the fuselage is half-hearted at best. The propeller spinners and the hub/pitch collar assemblies are inaccurate and underdetailed. The tail wheel is noticeably undersized and the wing tips are too squared-off. The 300l drop tank is puny and the over-long wing mounts amplify this impression. Smaller parts, such as the antennas and DF loop, lack the finesse of a more modern kit.

So, does this list of errors and omissions imply a bad kit? In my opinion, no.

With a little extra effort, Fujimi's 1/48-scale Messerschmitt Bf 110 can be transformed into a fine replica of this significant aircraft. Furthermore, it is still the only Messerschmitt Bf 110C/D kit available in this scale.

Messerschmitt Bf 110D on a stick

Intermediate Modelling Project
Built and painted by Brett Green
Additional weathering by Chris Wauchop

Although many model kits released around the 1960s included display stands, it is relatively rare to see a scale model depicted 'in flight' today. However, with the growing enthusiasm for wooden and die-cast presentation models, I predict a comeback for the plastic kit display stand.

I wanted to build Fujimi's Bf 110C/D almost straight from the box with minimal added detail. Building the model in-flight would not only be an interesting way to display the model, it would also bypass two of the major problem areas – the poor cockpit and minimal wheel well detail – because both the canopy and the landing gear doors would be closed.

Construction

Any in-flight model needs a pilot. I sourced two crew figures from Tamiya fighter kits. The sad blobs supplied in the Fujimi kit would hardly stand up to scrutiny even through the heavily framed plastic of the closed canopy.

The cockpit was assembled and painted Gunze H70 RLM 02 Grey, followed by a wash of thinned Winsor and Newton Raw Umber oil paint. The featureless plastic instrument panel was replaced with a leftover item from a True Details resin cockpit set. The figures were glued into place, small strips of masking tape were used to join the pilot's shoulder harness to the seat, and the fuselage was secured with liquid glue.

The biggest single modification to the model was closing the undercarriage doors. Test fitting showed that the doors were both too wide and too long for the undercarriage bay opening. They were therefore trimmed and glued in place. Large quantities of putty and associated sanding delivered a smooth result. The lost panel lines for the undercarriage doors were rescribed and locating holes for the 900l drop tanks were drilled before the wing halves were joined.

The fit of the remaining parts was excellent. A feed line was added to the 900l drop tanks, which were assembled on their mounts but not fitted to the aircraft until after painting.

ABOVE Fujimi's venerable 1/48-scale Messerschmitt Bf 110C/D kit is quite accurate and can be made into a very respectable replica even straight from the box.

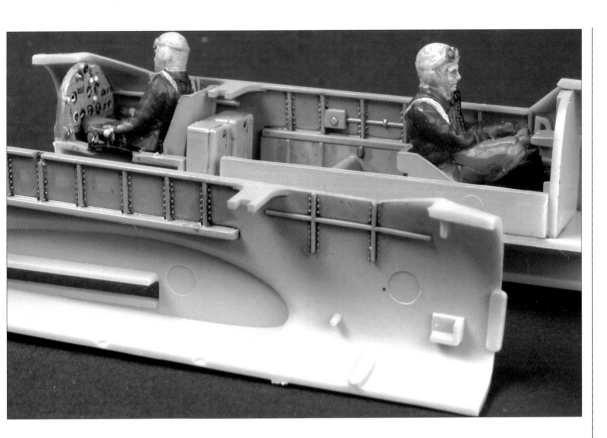

ABOVE The Fujimi Bf 110C was built almost straight from the box. The very bare cockpit is obvious in this view. Crew figures were sourced from two Tamiya kits. The resin instrument panel was left over from a True Details Bf 110 cockpit. The cockpit was sprayed RLM 02 Grey followed by a thin oil wash of Winsor and Newton Raw Umber.

BELOW The biggest modification was closing the undercarriage doors. The kit was obviously never designed to be depicted with the wheels up, as the doors were far too big to close. The contours of the doors were also quite different to the corresponding sections of the wheel well. The only answer was lots of measuring, cutting, filling and sanding. The large quantities of putty required can be seen here.

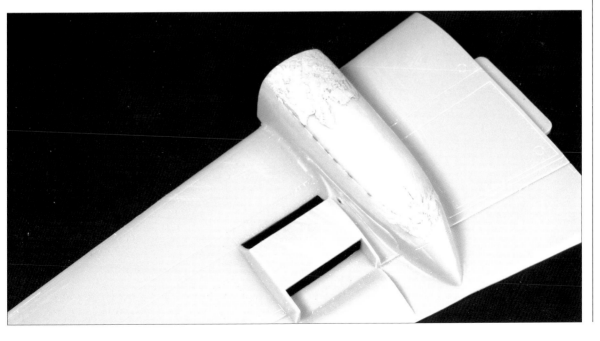

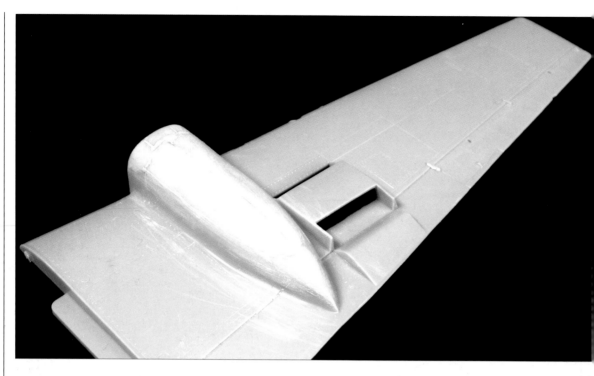

ABOVE Eventually, the doors were made to fit without gaps or steps.

BELOW The remainder of this old kit fitted very well. Locating holes were drilled for the 900l drop tanks. An additional hole was drilled in the centre to accommodate the fuel line.

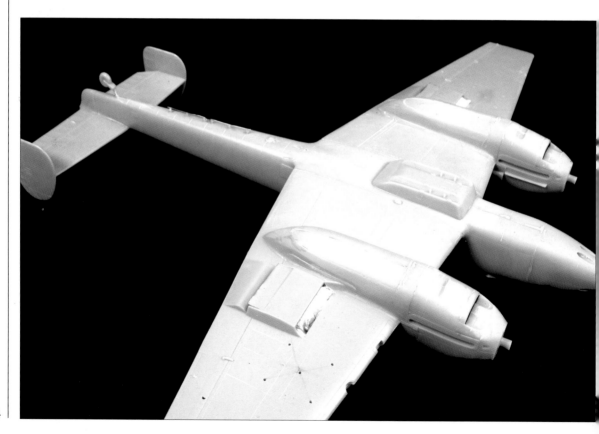

Painting and Markings

Famous Aircraft of the World No. 41: *Messerschmitt Bf 110*, has an excellent full-page photograph on page 10 of a Bf 110D in flight over the Mediterranean during the summer of 1941.

This aircraft is fitted with 900l drop tanks that are partially painted with a very dark colour about the same shade as the spinner and significantly darker than the other camouflage colours. I believe that the upper surface colours are most likely RLM 71 Dark Green and RLM 02 Grey. The new RLM 74/75/76 grey camouflage was in service at this stage, but the very low contrast between the paler upper camouflage colour and the paint on the lower surface suggests the earlier interim scheme was still being used on this aircraft. The colour on the drop tank is most likely RLM 70 Black Green.

A yellow code letter and spinner tips were supplemented with a yellow patch on the rudder, and two pieces of nose art completed this interesting package.

Fast Frames by True Details were used to mask the complex glasshouse. These are not masks, but self-adhesive vinyl canopy frames. The frames were sprayed while still on their white backing sheet.

The lower surfaces of the airframe were painted Gunze RLM 76 Light Blue. The real aircraft was probably painted RLM 65, a slightly deeper shade, but RLM 76 is a good representation of slightly faded lower surfaces. Gunze H70 RLM 02

The bottom of the model was sprayed with Gunze acrylic RLM 76 Light Blue. It is quite likely that the real aircraft wore the slightly deeper colour, RLM 65, but the lighter shade seemed to be a good representation for weather-worn lower surfaces.

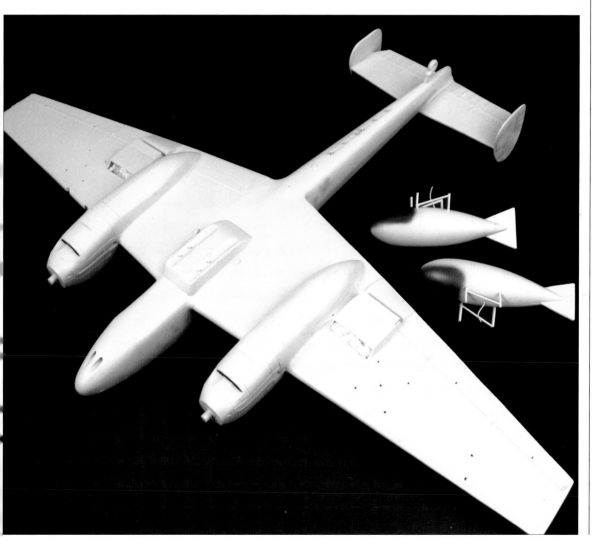

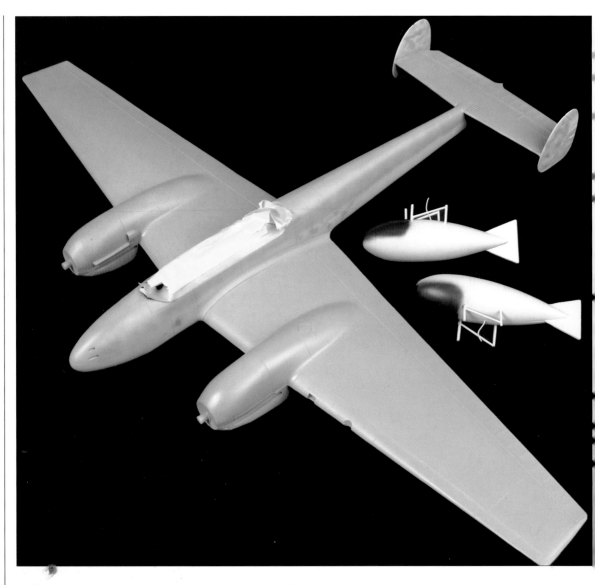

References for this aircraft suggest that it was painted in RLM 74 Grey Green and RLM 75 Grey Violet on the upper surfaces. However, the camouflage pattern, the date of the reference photographs and the contrast between the colours leads me to believe that the camouflage may have been the interim scheme of RLM 02 Grey and RLM 71 Dark Green. Furthermore, the top of the drop tanks seem to be painted a darker colour, similar to the colour on the spinners – probably RLM 70 Black Green.

Grey was applied to the upper surface and down to the mid fuselage. This colour was also used for mottling the fuselage sides and fins.

Black Magic masks were used as a guide for the camouflage pattern. The masks were gently laid over the RLM 02 colour. A fine line of Gunze H64 RLM 71 Dark Green was sprayed close to the edges of the masks before the black vinyl sheets were removed. The empty spaces between the lines were then filled in freehand with the airbrush. The camouflage on the fuselage did not seem to conform to a standard pattern, so it was sprayed entirely freehand. The white fuselage band was masked and sprayed with Tamiya XF-2 Flat White.

Panel lines were highlighted with a combination of pencil, thin semi-gloss black wash and subtle overspraying with the airbrush.

Decals were sourced from Superscale sheet number 48-25. This is an old release and the instructions reflected the common beliefs about Luftwaffe camouflage colours of the era. However, the decals themselves were not bad even though the shape of the font and the rooster did not completely match the styles seen in the photographs. They performed flawlessly on application despite their age, with the thin decals settling down perfectly in the panel lines.

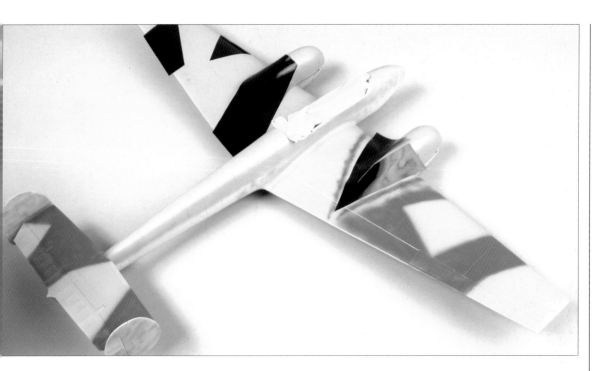

ABOVE The bottom of the model was sprayed with Gunze acrylic RLM 76 Light Blue. It is quite likely that the real aircraft wore the slightly deeper colour, RLM 65, but the lighter shade seemed to be a good representation for weather-worn lower surfaces. Black Magic self-adhesive camouflage masks were used as a guide for the camouflage pattern. The masks were stuck to the wings and tailplanes, over the base coat of RLM 02 Grey. I then sprayed a fine line close to the edge of the masks before removing them and 'filling in' the darker camouflage colour (RLM 71 Dark Green). The camouflage on the fuselage was sprayed freehand, as it did not appear to conform to the standard camouflage pattern supplied as masks.

The white Mediterranean theatre fuselage band was masked and sprayed after the camouflage was applied.

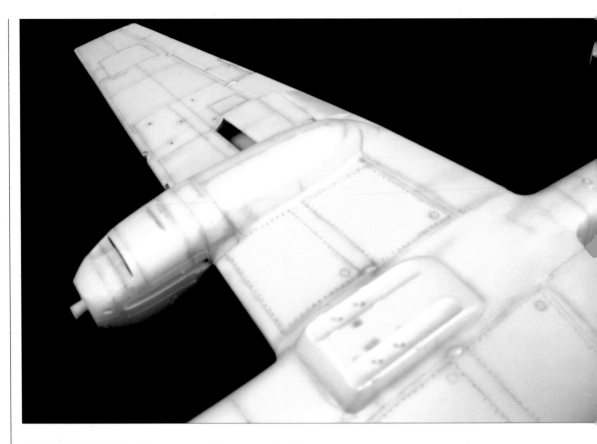

ABOVE AND BELOW Panel lines were carefully sprayed with a thin
mix of brown and black.

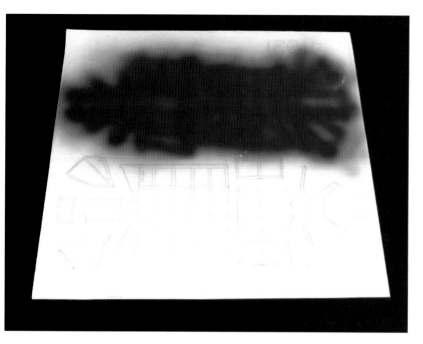

Fast Frames were used for the canopy on this model. These are not painting masks. They are self-adhesive, clear vinyl frames that become a permanent part of your model. The Fast Frames are first painted in the interior colour (RLM 02 in this case), followed by a coat of the upper camouflage colour (RLM 71 Dark Green). The frames are then very carefully lifted from the backing sheet. The vinyl can stretch, and this will affect the fit, so time and care is required.

The frames should be quickly dipped in soapy water before being applied to the canopy. This adds some free play if adjustment is required. Apart from some complications around the thick armour-plated windscreen, the Fast Frames were very effective.

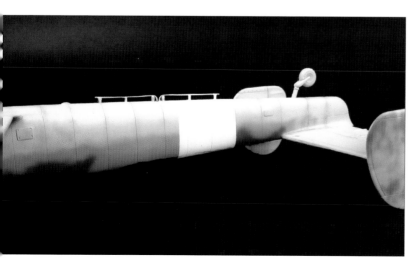

The kit FuG1 2F antenna was replaced with fine brass wire.

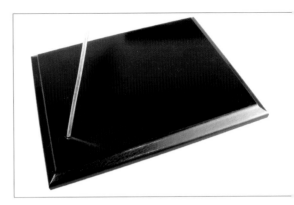

ABOVE Some of the final details ready to add after the airframe has been painted and weathered.

ABOVE RIGHT The stand is a 25cm x 20cm wooden plaque. The mount is aluminium tube. A diagonal hole was drilled in the lower fuselage of the kit for mounting.

BELOW The Fujimi Bf 110D on its stand.

Detail parts, including the drop tanks and propeller assemblies, were added before a final coat of Polly Scale acrylic flat. The canopy and aerial masts were then glued on, wing tip lights painted, aerial wire added from invisible mending thread and the model was almost complete.

The base was a black wooden plaque. A diagonal hole was drilled in one corner and fitted with 50mm aluminium tubing. Prior to painting, the lower fuselage was drilled out to accept this tube. The model is quite secure, and it can be set in various positions on the stand.

With the crew figures installed and the model elevated from the base, it made sense to photograph this Bf 110 in flight. Technology has given us a number of options for creating the illusion of flight by blurring the propellers in photographs. These options include small electric motors and computer graphics programs.

However, I opted for a low-tech approach.

The spinners were not glued to the plastic propeller shaft during construction. Care was also taken to ensure that the propellers would spin freely when the assemblies were in place.

With the model painted and mounted on its stand, I placed the kit in front of a blue-sky photographic background, set up my digital camera on a tripod, set the self-timer and pointed a hairdryer at the front of the model.

After some experimentation, I found a reliable angle from which the air spun both propellers at high speed. At that point it was a simple matter of taking photos at a number of different angles.

Before you try this technique yourself, make sure that the hairdryer has the option of turning off the heat, otherwise the propeller blades might melt instead of spin!

I used a graphics program, Adobe Photoshop Elements, to edit out the metal stand. The same program was used to copy one photo of the model and modify the codes (and a few other details) to create the additional aircraft '3U+MT' in the background of one of these photos.

ABOVE The model in formation flight – thanks to Adobe Photoshop!

BELOW The big 900l drop tanks make an unmistakable impression on the profile of the slim Messerschmitt Bf 110. The uncorrected mounts are a little long on the kit, resulting in the tanks sitting lower and further exaggerating their size. The overly large openings in the spinners are obvious in this photo.

*Advanced Modelling Project
Built and painted by
Brett Green
Additional weathering by
Chris Wauchop*

Back in black – a Messerschmitt Bf 110E night fighter

There are relatively few aftermarket accessories available for Fujimi's 1/48-scale Messerschmitt Bf 110C/D. Even so, I wanted to make some significant improvements to the model for this project.

Cockpit

True Details had a 1/48-scale Messerschmitt Bf 110C/D resin cockpit in their range during the 1990s. It is no longer in production but many should still be in circulation. The replacement cockpit is made up of ten pieces in pale-coloured resin. Although the breakdown of parts is quite simple, this set vastly improves the kit cockpit with good sidewall detail, a cannon installed in the new floor and good seats with harnesses moulded on.

The kit fuselage sidewalls were prepared by grinding off the raised detail and locator tabs with a Dremel motor tool. Checking the resin sidewall against the kit fuselage showed that the resin parts were drooping at the front. This would affect the fit, so the front of the resin sidewalls were cut off and repositioned on the fuselage interior. A small gap behind each cut was plugged with styrene strip.

Most of True Details's parts were very good, but the instrument panel was oversimplified. I used the photo-etched instrument panel from Eduard detail set no. 48-253 instead. This is an extensive photo-etched detail set with many useful parts to improve the Fujimi kit.

The Eduard radio panel was also employed, but this part was too flat to use without modification. The panel was supplemented with five blocks of styrene cut to shape, and a circular section sliced from a wooden paintbrush handle to act as the base for the prominent direction finder display. The radio faces were glued to the boxes, and hexagonal knobs were punched from a Historex punch and die set.

The detail was now brought out of the cockpit components with careful painting. The cockpit was painted in the following stages:

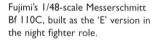

Fujimi's 1/48-scale Messerschmitt Bf 110C, built as the 'E' version in the night fighter role.

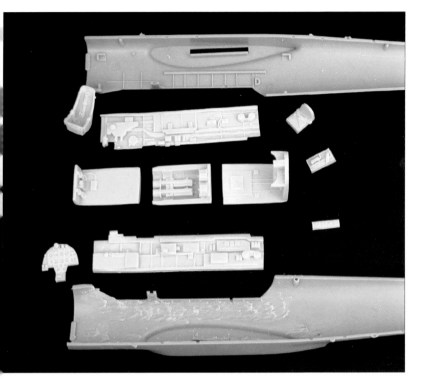

The True Detail Messerschmitt Bf 110C/D cockpit components can be seen here. The breakdown of the parts is simple but the detail is quite good, representing a vast improvement over the kit parts. Structural detail on the inside of the fuselage halves must be removed before the resin parts can be fitted. The sidewall detail and locating points have already been ground off the starboard fuselage half (bottom) using a Dremel motor tool.

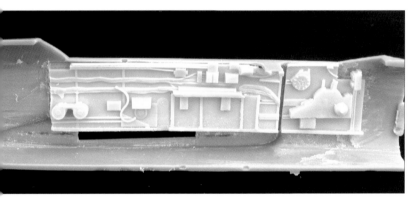

Both resin sidewalls were warped, resulting in a droop at the front that would interfere with the fit of the floor. The front part of each sidewall was cut off and repositioned on the kit fuselage. The gap was filled with a narrow strip of plastic.

1. All cockpit parts were sprayed with a coat of flat black. This black paint acts as a 'shadow coat', and shows through the lighter top colour in undercuts and recesses as darker areas.
2. Next, Gunze H70 RLM 02 was sprayed at a constant downward angle to retain some of the black in naturally shaded areas.
3. A thin wash of black oil paint was applied to the painted interior and left to dry overnight.
4. When the cockpit was dry, a finger dipped in turpentine was rubbed over the high points of the cockpit to remove excess wash. This increased the contrast between the shadow areas and the high points.
5. Structural details such as cabling, hoses, throttles and knobs were brush painted using Tamiya acrylics. Harness straps were painted with Tamiya XF-55 Deck Tan.
6. The harnesses received a further, carefully applied wash of thinned Winsor and Newton Burnt Umber oil paint to add depth.

The cockpit parts were assembled and fitted inside the fuselage

RIGHT Test fitting showed that there would be no major problems when the time came to join the fuselage halves.

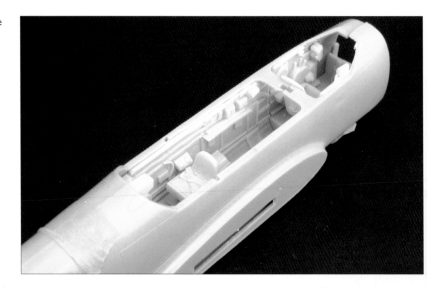

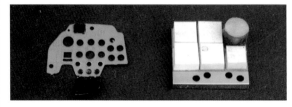

ABOVE The resin cockpit was supplemented with parts from Eduard photo-etched detail set No. 48-253. I did not like the resin instrument panel supplied with the True Details set, so I used the Eduard item. The photo-etched radio looked too two-dimensional, so I added small blocks of plastic plus a cross section of a wooden paintbrush handle as the base for the direction finder display.

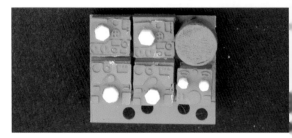

ABOVE Knobs were also added to the radio. These were punched from scrap plastic using a Historex hexagonal punch and die set.

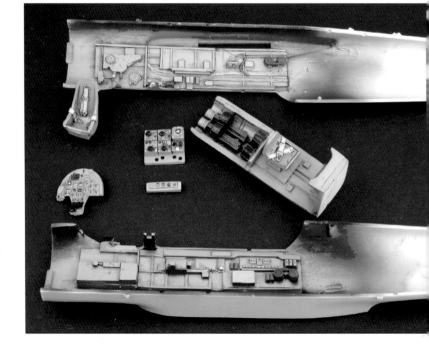

RIGHT The cockpit components were painted before assembly. A thin coat of RLM 02 Grey was sprayed over black paint. A wash of black oil paint, heavily thinned with turpentine, was applied to the basic interior colour. After leaving the parts to dry overnight, the details were picked out with a fine brush using acrylic paints.

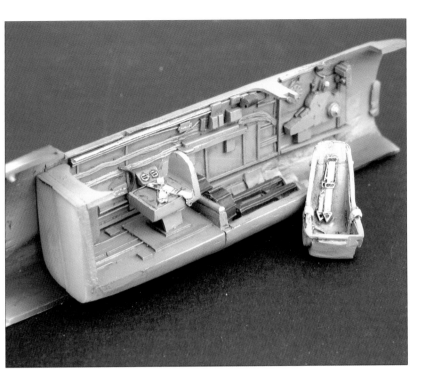

LEFT The resin fuselage floor was glued to one sidewall before the fuselage halves were joined.

Airframe detailing and construction

The fuselage halves were glued, taped and clamped. The fit at the top panel lines was quite good, but alignment along the bottom of the fuselage was poor.

In the meantime, the wings were readied for resin flaps and leading edge slats.

Highflight Replicas used to produce a set of flaps for the Fujimi kit and I had a set stashed away. No company ever released slats for this kit though, so I had to scratch-build these items. The panel lines for the slats and the flaps were removed by repeated scoring with a sharp knife. Particular care was required when separating the slats because I planned to use the plastic that had been removed as the dropped slats after further modification. Once the plastic was detached, the trailing edges of the upper and lower wings were thinned where they would join the flaps. This task was especially tricky around the back of the wheel well.

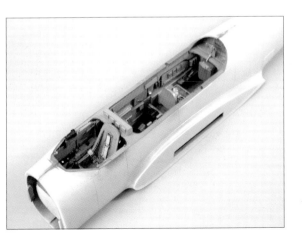

ABOVE The True Details resin and Eduard brass made a huge difference to the long, exposed cockpit.

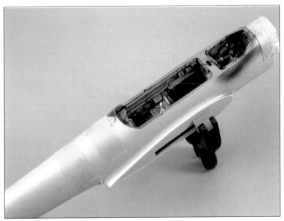

ABOVE The fuselage halves were taped and clamped while drying.

25

RIGHT The kit wings were prepared for resin flaps from Highflight Replicas and scratch-built leading edge slats. The panel lines for slats and flaps were scored with a sharp hobby knife and the plastic was removed. I took care to keep the slats intact, as these sections would be adapted for use in the deployed (dropped) position. The trailing edges of the upper and lower wings needed to be thinned where they were to join the flaps. This was especially tricky around the rear of the wheel well. Constant test fitting of the flaps was required.

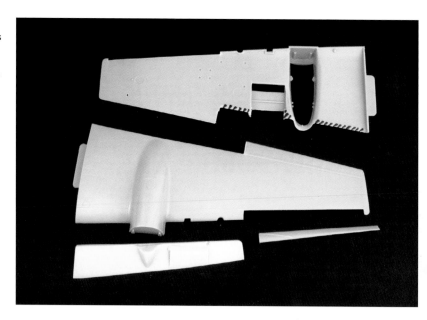

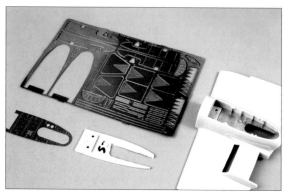

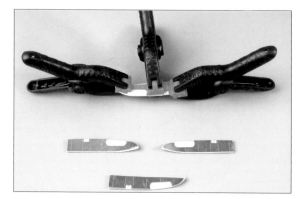

ABOVE AND ABOVE RIGHT The Fujimi kit wheel wells are completely devoid of detail. Eduard photo-etched parts were added for supports and ceiling features. The kit wheel well ceiling is solid plastic. It was modified to allow for the cavity for the main wheel. Multiple clamps were used to secure the gear door interiors.

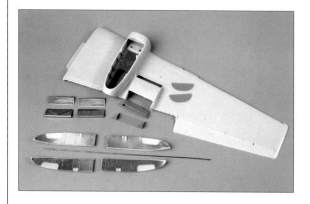

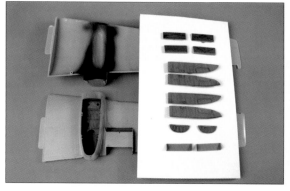

ABOVE Eduard brass was also used for radiator faces, radiator flaps and oil cooler faces.

ABOVE Wheel well and exterior detail parts were painted using the same technique as the cockpit – a thorough base coat of black followed by RLM 02 Grey and, finally, a black oil wash.

ABOVE AND ABOVE RIGHT The brass radiator faces were further detailed with diagonal
strips of brass wire and a thicker piece of brass rod as an actuator for the front radiator flap.

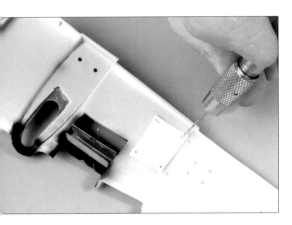 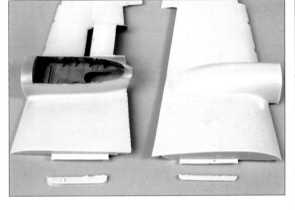

ABOVE The 300l drop tanks were to be replaced by the more
accurate items in the ProModeler Bf 110G kit, so new locating
holes needed to be drilled.

A piece of paper was laid over the locating holes for the drop
tank rack in the ProModeler wing and the positions were
marked. This paper was laid over the corresponding positions on
the Fujimi kit wings and was used as a template to drill holes that
were correctly spaced for the ProModeler drop tank racks.

ABOVE The deep replacement resin floor interfered with the
locating tabs on the wings. The tabs were sliced shorter to
permit the wings to fit snugly against the wing roots.

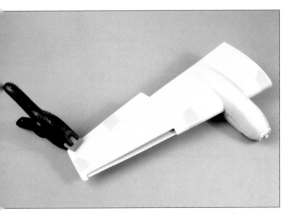 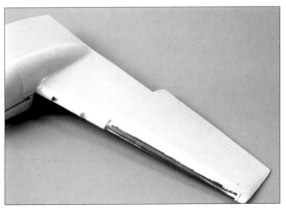

ABOVE AND ABOVE RIGHT The wing halves were glued, taped and clamped. The engine nacelles
were also added at this time. Lengths of aerofoil section plastic were used as inserts on which to
mount the leading edge slats. Fitting these parts and obtaining a gap-free fit proved quite tricky!

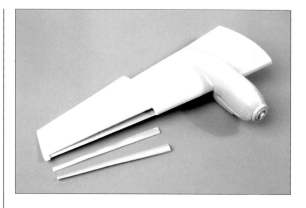

ABOVE The starboard wing, the insert and the slats, ready for assembly.

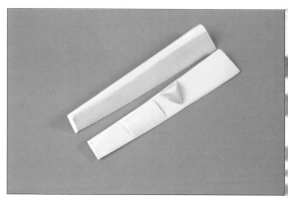

ABOVE The Highflight flaps were not quite long enough for the space left in the wing. The shortfall was made up with scrap plastic.

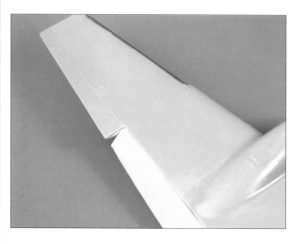

ABOVE Small gaps between the inside surfaces of the aileron halves were filled with Milliput two-part epoxy putty. The flaps were then secured using super glue.

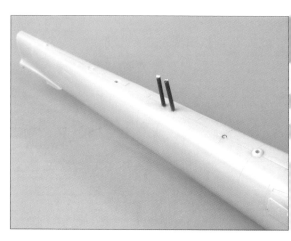

ABOVE The large holes in the bottom of the fuselage for the FuG1 2F antenna were filled with plastic rod.

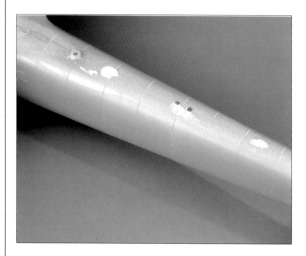

ABOVE The rods were cut off flush with the surface of the kit then puttied to achieve a smooth finish. The overscale FuG1 2F kit antenna was replaced with a photo-etched part from the Eduard set.

ABOVE The fit of the fuselage was poor on this model. Plenty of filler was required to level a serious step along the centreline of the fuselage.

ABOVE The fit of the boat tail and the tailplanes also needed putty and sanding.

ABOVE The contour of the lower nose should be smooth, but the Fujimi kit features a distinct angle between the forward fuselage and the nose cap. The shaded area in the picture (and the corresponding area on the other side of the nose) was sanded to deliver a more accurate, smoother contour.

ABOVE A rectangular cooling vent was added to the front of the gun cowling on the Messerschmitt Bf 110E. This small vent was cut from thin sheet brass and folded into shape. It was glued to the nose using super glue and faired-in with Mr Surfacer.

ABOVE The 300l drop tanks from the ProModeler kit were added at this stage. The leading edge slats were glued on too.

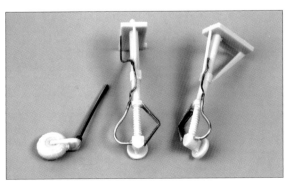

ABOVE In the interests of a more robust join, the tail wheel assembly was cut off the fuselage and the tail wheel strut was replaced with a length of brass rod. The main undercarriage legs were detailed with oleo scissors from the Eduard set and brake lines from an industrial light filament.

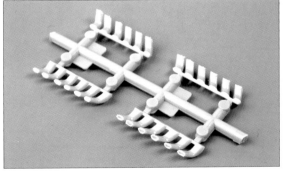

ABOVE Exhaust stacks were drilled out with a dental burr fitted to the Dremel motor tool.

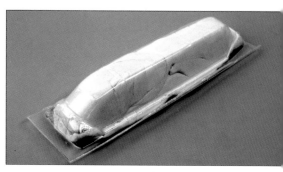

ABOVE Some other small details include an outstandingly detailed MG15 machine gun from Cavalier with an Eduard brass ring gunsight; a Revi C/12D gunsight from Cutting Edge and a scratch-built pitot tube from brass tube and copper wire.

ABOVE A Falcon vacform canopy was used for this model. This was mainly to permit the clamshell rear canopy to be opened, which would be impossible using the thick plastic parts supplied in the kit. The flimsy vacform part was packed with BluTack to provide support while it was being sliced away from the sheet.

RIGHT Once free of its backing sheet, the clear parts were masked using strips of Tamiya masking tape cut to size.

RIGHT All the parts were backed with masking tape and smaller parts were secured to a small pad.

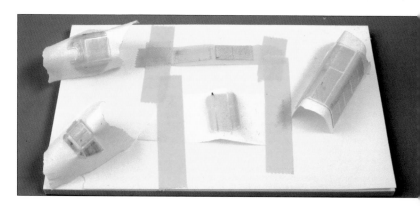

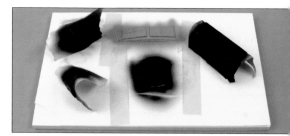

ABOVE The first paint coat was Gunze RLM 02, representing the colour of the aircraft interior.

ABOVE Next came the black camouflage colour.

The vacant wheel wells were improved with parts from the Eduard detail set. First, though, the wheel well ceilings (parts 53 and 57) were opened up to depict the cavities for the main wheels. Photo-etched parts were used for the gear bay supports and ceilings, and to add detail to the interior of the undercarriage doors. Parts from the Eduard set were also used for the radiator faces, the rear radiator flaps and the oil cooler faces. Brass rod was used to detail the photo-etched radiator faces and as actuators for the front radiator flaps.

The Fujimi drop tanks are noticeably undersized. They were substituted with a set of 300l tanks from the Revell-Monogram kit. The Revell mounts were also used. The different mounts required different locating hole positions so a template was made by laying a piece of paper over the locating holes in the Revell wing and marking the positions with a small hole. The template was then laid on the inside of the Fujimi lower wings and drilled though. These holes were now correctly positioned for the Revell drop tanks.

The wings were taped together and checked for fit against the fuselage. The resin True Details floor covered the inside of the locating slots, so the wing tabs were cut shorter. The wing halves were now glued together.

Mounts for the leading edge slats aerofoil were cut from Contrail aerofoil struts. The struts were sanded flat on the bottom then installed. A great deal of fiddling, trimming, sanding and filling was required before the inserts looked sensible. In hindsight, this little project would have been easier if I had glued the inserts to the top wing before gluing the wing halves together.

The resin Highflight flaps were slightly short compared to the gap in the back of the wing. Scrap styrene strip was used to lengthen the flaps. Small gaps between the top and the bottom of the inside edge of the aileron were filled with Milliput two-part epoxy putty.

Several hours were spent filling and sanding the various gaps and steps around the airframe. The biggest problem areas were the lower-mid fuselage and the top of the horizontal tailplanes. The contour of the lower nose was also smoothed with a sanding stick.

The sole unique external identifying factor of a Bf 110E is a rectangular cooling vent in the centre of the top gun cowl. I cut a piece of thin sheet brass and folded it into the approximate shape of the vent. The piece was fixed to the nose using super glue and faired in with Mr Surfacer. As it turns out, I did not really get the shape right. I depicted the top as almost horizontal whereas it should have more of a downward slope.

Smaller details were prepared:

- Revell's drop tanks were fitted.
- The tail wheel strut was replaced with brass rod.
- The main gear legs were detailed with hydraulic lines from industrial light filament.
- Exhaust stacks were drilled out.
- A pitot tube was scratch-built from brass tube and copper wire.
- Eduard's brass gunsight was added to a resin MG15 machine gun from a Luftwaffe weapons set by Cavalier.
- The Cutting Edge resin Revi C/12D gunsight was painted.

The rear canopy of early Bf 110s featured an interesting clamshell rear hatch. This was split into a main part that hinged back into the canopy, and a upper section that slid over the top of the canopy. I sliced up the kit canopy, but there was no way that the thick plastic parts could be authentically positioned. I therefore used a Falcon vacform canopy.

The Falcon canopy was cut from its base and masked with strips of Tamiya masking tape before being sprayed.

ABOVE The cockpit opening was masked in preparation for paint.

ABOVE RIGHT The wheel wells were masked with Tamiya tape, while the oil cooler intakes were plugged with BluTack. Note that the ETC rack from ProModeler's Bf 110G-2 kit has been fitted. The match to Fujimi's lower fuselage was not too bad. A gap-free fit was achieved after a little trimming and fairing in with Mr Surfacer.

RIGHT The entire airframe received a coat of 'scale black'. This is a mix of 50 per cent Tamiya Flat Black and 50 per cent Tamiya Red Brown. This colour looks like black in most circumstances, but it permits additional weathering and panel variation using 100 per cent black.

Painting and markings

The canopy, wheel wells and other openings were masked in preparation for painting.

The entire airframe received a coat of 'scale black'. This is a mix of 50 per cent Tamiya XF-1 Flat Black and 50 per cent Tamiya Red Brown. This colour looks black under most circumstances, but it permits more options for weathering.

Panel lines and hatches were highlighted with 100 per cent Flat Black. Exhaust stains applied with Tamiya acrylics are an important way to add some variation to the uniformly dark finish. Tamiya acrylic Buff was mixed with a small blob of Tamiya Flat Base, then thinned with around 70 per cent isopropylene alcohol. This watery mix was sprayed as very fine lines, built up gradually over multiple coats. The result is a chalky stain typical of a lean-running engine.

LEFT Panel lines and hatches are outlined with 100 per cent Tamiya Flat Black applied with an airbrush. The contrast between shaded panel lines and the 'scale black' mix on the wing is obvious in this photograph. The exhaust stain has been sprayed using a mix of Tamiya acrylics.

BELOW The addition of decals, panel line highlighting and exhaust stains breaks up the potentially monotonous uniform finish.

Wing walkway chipping was applied with the point of a sharp silver artists' pencil.

Smoke-coloured nylon mending thread was inserted through a small hole drilled into the fuselage. This is the lead-in wire that will eventually be attached to the main aerial wire between the mast and the fin. The photo-etched direction finder loop under the fuselage is also visible in this photo. Note the four small white plastic blocks along the rim of the cockpit opening. These acted as spacers and supports for the vacform canopy

Decals were sourced from AeroMaster sheet no. 48-066. The artwork on the decal instructions displays a toned-down shark's mouth, the night fighter badge on the nose and a row of campaign flags under the canopy. However, I could not find any evidence that this aircraft carried all these markings and seeing there was not enough room for both the night fighter badge and the shark's mouth to fit on the nose together, I omitted the shark's mouth.

Wing walkway chipping was applied with the point of a sharp silver artists' pencil. Wing roots of World War II aircraft were often chipped and scuffed from the boots of the crewmembers and service personnel. This chipping can easily be replicated by applying tiny spots and 'scratches' with the point of a sharp silver artist's pencil. The pattern should be most heavily applied to the areas with the greatest traffic, generally the wing root close to the fuselage.

Finishing touches

The final touches to complete the model included:

- Fixing four spacer blocks to the rim of the cockpit opening. These were used to support and position the flexible vacform canopy.
- The installation of spacer blocks at the back of the main undercarriage leg mounting plates. These styrene spacers forced the angle of the gear legs slightly forward.
- Wing formation lights painted to represent clear parts. This is an alternative to the otherwise time consuming chore of cutting out the solid plastic outlines of the lights and replacing them with clear stock. Instead, I painted inside the outline of the formation light on each wing tip using grey acrylic paint. When this was dry, an oval of white paint was added to the front corner of each light. Finally, Tamiya Clear Red and Gunze Clear Green were painted over the port and starboard navigation lights respectively. The object of painting the grey and white is to create the impression that the lens cover is transparent.

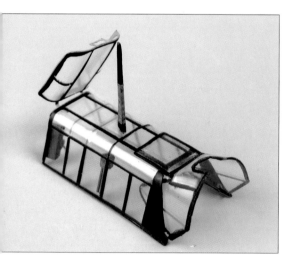

ABOVE The rear section of the vacform canopy is ready to be fitted. Note the unusual arrangement of the rear hatch, with its clamshell section tilting back into the main canopy and the separate section sliding over the top.

ABOVE The kit landing gear rests at 90° to the horizontal, whereas the legs should lean slightly forward. A plastic spacer has been added to back of the undercarriage mounting plates to force the gear legs slightly forward.

ABOVE Formation lights are moulded as part of the wing, represented only by scribed lines. The outline of the lights was painted in dark grey, then a teardrop shape was painted in white.

ABOVE When the grey and white is overpainted with Tamiya Clear Red (on the port side) and Gunze Clear Green (on the starboard), it creates the illusion that the lens is transparent.

The two seated figures are white metal castings from Andrea Miniatures. The figure donning his life vest is from Airwaves. All three figures are presented in 1/48 scale.

Conclusion

This Messerschmitt Bf 110E is far from perfect, but it does demonstrate the potential to improve the kit with a little extra work. The installation of the cockpit alone makes an enormous difference.

There are not many 30-year-old kits that would justify this level of attention but, in my opinion, Fujimi's Bf 110 is worth the effort.

The dropped landing flaps break up the shape of the wings.

Building the Revell-Monogram family of Messerschmitt Bf 110s

Revell's Messerschmitt Bf 110G in the box

Depending on the variant, Revell-Monogram's family of Bf 110G kits have either 119 or 120 parts in grey plastic, and an additional 14 parts in clear plastic.

Three versions of the Bf 110 in 1/48 scale were released by Revell-Monogram. The three share four sprues with all the major parts. The unique sprue for the Bf 110G-4 night fighter kit includes radar, flame-damper exhausts and 30mm cannon nose; the Bf 110G-2 kit has this sprue substituted with one containing four W.Gr42 air-to-air rockets, a *Rustatz* M1 ventral gun pack with two 20mm cannon, a tropical air filter and a different nose with the upper cannon ports blanked off. The third boxing, also a Bf 110G-2, supplies colourful markings for ZG 1 and includes a resin nose with machine gun armament. This kit is otherwise identical to the other Bf 110G-2 boxing.

The kits are very impressive in the box. Panel lines are crisply recessed and fabric texture on control surfaces is well done. The cockpit, wheel wells, drop tanks, ETC bomb rack and undercarriage legs are all very well detailed.

Surprisingly, this recently released kit suffers from some flash on the sprues, but this thin excess plastic is easily cleaned up prior to construction. There is also a moulding flaw on the upper-mid fuselage taking the form of a few shallow depressions in the plastic. This flaw was worst on the very earliest kits and caused howls of outrage on release. Later mouldings were better, but the flaw is still evident. Luckily, correcting the defect is quick and easy.

The outline and dimensions of the kit are generally good, but there is one major discrepancy and a few minor problems.

The biggest problem is the size and shape of the engine nacelles and spinners. Although the length of each nacelle is correct, the height is not. It is several millimetres short. The undersized nacelle translates to the diameter of the spinner. The 2mm difference in this area is quite noticeable. The problem is also telegraphed to the hump on the wing behind the engine nacelle. It, too, is not quite high enough and does not extend as far back as it should.

The next noticeable fault is the angle of the main undercarriage legs. They are raked too far forward. Unlike the engine nacelle, this is a fairly easy problem to correct.

The final issue relates to a case of mistaken identity. Revell's kit labelled 'Messerschmitt Bf 110G-2' is, in fact, a Bf 110F-2. The under-wing pitot tube supplied in the kit singles out the kit as the F variant. However, conversion back to a G-2 is as simple as installing a new pitot tube on the starboard wingtip.

In summary, Revell-Monogram's Messerschmitt Bf 110G kits are attractive, well detailed models. Many modellers will not be concerned about the inaccurate engine nacelles and spinners, but others will want to address this problem.

In the next two chapters, we will build one Messerschmitt Bf 110G-4 almost straight from the box, and a second with major corrections and detailing.

Dressing up a Messerschmitt Bf 110G-4

*Intermediate Project
Built, Painted and Weathered
by Chris Wauchop*

For this project, ProModeler's 1/48-scale Messerschmitt Bf 110G-4 was built with only minor corrections and detailing. The objective of this undertaking was to take full advantage of kit detail by careful painting and weathering.

Construction

Construction started with the cockpit. The breakdown of parts in this area is quite simple, but detail is excellent. The only additions to this area were harnesses cut from thin lead foil. Buckles were bent from fine wire that had been unravelled from 6-strand picture wire.

Painting of the cockpit began with a base coat of Tamiya XF-24 Dark Grey. This colour is significantly lighter than the very dark RLM 66 that featured in the real aircraft. The airbrush was next loaded with a thin mix of Tamiya XF-1 Flat Black and XF-64 Red Brown to add depth and shadows to this relatively pale base colour. It is important that the paint mix is very thin – almost a wash with the consistency of water. Narrow lines of this thin mix were sprayed very carefully around cockpit structural features to depict shaded areas, and streaked along larger surfaces to suggest grime.

The woven rear seat was painted Tamiya XF-57 Buff, followed by a wash of thinned black paint placed around each woven strip with a fine brush. When the seat was dry, the brown/black mix was airbrushed along the strips to confer the impression of depth to the flat plastic parts.

Instrument faces were painted gloss black to suggest clear lenses. Dial details were picked out in white using a 10/0 brush. Other details in the cockpit area, such as electrical wiring, hydraulic cables, throttle quadrants, knobs and hoses, were also brush-painted at this time. The large breeches of the 20mm cannon installed in the floor were painted flat black, then burnished with a 2B pencil.

Wheel well detail is impressive without enhancement. It was decided to paint this portion of the kit before the parts were removed from the sprue in order to get easier access to the recesses of the wheel wells. All undercarriage parts, including the gear doors and legs, received a coat of Gunze H70 RLM 02 Grey. This was immediately followed by a wash of thinned semi-gloss black paint around the raised details. The wash was not slopped over the whole vicinity, but carefully delivered to the areas requiring attention, minimizing drying time and clean-up. The final step was a carefully airbrushed application of the Tamiya Black/Brown mix in shadow areas, along the edges of supports and the rows of rivets.

ProModeler's 1/48-scale Messerschmitt Bf 110G-4 built almost straight from the box.

ABOVE All the kit cockpit parts were used, with only a few simple additions. Harnesses were cut from thin lead foil with buckles from fine wire, unravelled from 6-strand picture wire.

ABOVE The instrument faces were painted gloss black. Dial detail was hand painted using Tamiya Flat White and a 10/0 brush. The woven rear seat was painted Tamiya Buff. A black wash was carefully placed around each woven strip then, when dry, the thin black/brown mix was sprayed to add further depth to the seat. Other cockpit details were picked out with a fine brush.

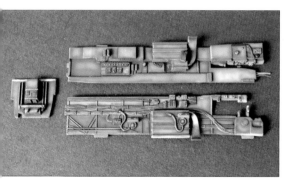

ABOVE All the cockpit components were first painted with Tamiya Dark Grey (XF-24). The airbrush was then loaded with a thin mix of Tamiya Flat Black (XF-1) and Red Brown (XF-64), which was applied carefully as shading and weathering.

The yellow wiring at the front of the top sidewall was added from fine wire.

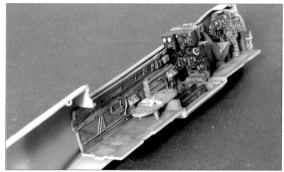

ABOVE Most of the cockpit components are seen here before the fuselage halves are joined. Kit detail really is very good. The 20mm cannon breeches in the floor were painted Tamiya Flat Black then burnished with a 2B pencil.

With the sub-assemblies painted, construction moved ahead quickly and without incident.

The only fit problem was a slight step at the lower join between the port and starboard wings. A line of Gunze Mr Surfacer was first applied along the ridge between the lower wings, and the remaining step was smoothed with a sanding stick.

The incorrectly angled supercharger intake was corrected before painting. The halves of the intake (kit parts 15 and 16) were glued together and, when thoroughly set, the intake pipe was cut off the base using a razor saw. The base was then glued to the engine nacelle, making it a simple task to reposition the pipe at the correct angle.

Shell ejector chutes below the nose were quite shallow, so they were hollowed out with a sharp scalpel blade. Additional details included a retaining strap for the

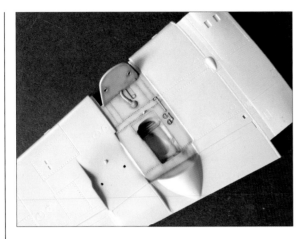

ABOVE The wheel well areas were painted with a base coat of Gunze acrylic RLM 02 followed by a wash of thinned semi-gloss black paint around raised detail. Structural features were finally sprayed with the thin black/brown mix.

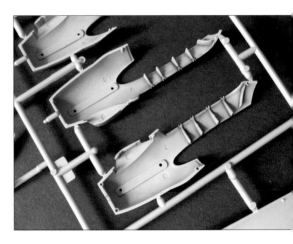

ABOVE The sidewalls of the main undercarriage bays received the same treatment as the top of the wheel wells. It is important that this weathering mix be sprayed very thiny and applied only in fine lines

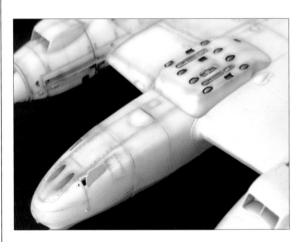

ABOVE Shell ejector chutes under the nose were hollowed out with a scalpel blade. A retaining strap for the shell deflector plate and dribble pipes in the oil cooler housings were added from stretched sprue.

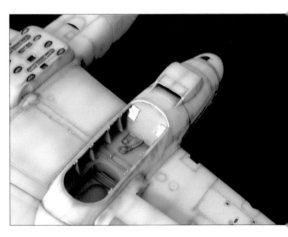

ABOVE Without modification, the kit undercarriage legs lean too far forward. The forward mounting holes for the gear legs were patched with plastic and new locating lugs were glued in a lower location to reposition the angle of the undercarriage. The semi-circular lugs were sliced from plastic tube and cut in half.

shell deflector plate, dribble tubes in the front of the nacelle-mounted oil cooler housings and actuator struts inside the radiators. All these parts were fabricated from stretched sprue.

Test fitting the undercarriage gear confirmed that the legs would be slanted too far forward using the locating holes in the front of the wheel wells. The existing holes were covered with plastic and new cradles for each forward locating pin were fabricated from slices of plastic tube cut in half. These cradles were glued in position below the old holes, effectively reducing the forward slant of the undercarriage legs.

Painting

The subject aircraft sported a typically simple late-war finish of RLM 76 Light Blue on the lower surfaces, and RLM 75 Grey Violet on the upper surfaces. Reference seemed ambiguous about whether this Bf 110G had a mottled fuselage, or whether there was a simple, high demarcation between the colours. In the end, a compromise was decided upon in the form of a very sparse mottle of RLM 75 Grey Violet over the RLM 76 fuselage sides.

There are many ways to approach painting and weathering.

This aircraft was destined to be post-shaded. Highlighting of structural details and weathering would be added after the basic camouflage colours were applied.

Gunze acrylic paints were used for both the camouflage colours. The Gunze RLM 75 looked too dark during test spraying, so it was lightened with around 15 per cent RLM 76 Light Blue.

The airbrush was the usual Aztek A470 fitted with the tan-coloured 'fine line' nozzle.

Cockpit and wheel well areas were masked before spraying the lower surfaces.

Demarcation lines at the wing roots and upper fuselage were not masked, they were sprayed freehand. Light mottling was also applied freehand on the fuselage sides.

At this stage the model looked quite bland. Post-shading added some character and depth to the paint job.

There is no single 'correct' method for post-shading, but this model was weathered using the following steps:

Weathering panel lines on pale colours

It is easy to overdo panel line shading under any circumstances, but it is especially risky over very pale colours such as RLM 76 Light Blue. A 2B clutch pencil was used to lightly draw along the panel lines and structural features on all the surfaces painted in RLM 76. This results in a more subtle effect than a wash of black paint and is also more forgiving, as an eraser can be used to remove any mistakes or heavy lines.

When the panel lines were drawn-in, they received a very thin airbrushed shading of a brown/black mix (Tamiya XF-1 and XF-64). In addition to panel lines, this thin mix can be sprayed into the crevices between nacelle and wing and the edges of the radiators and oil coolers.

Always keep in mind that the emphasis is on subtlety, so make sure that the airbrush paint mix is very thin – almost transparent.

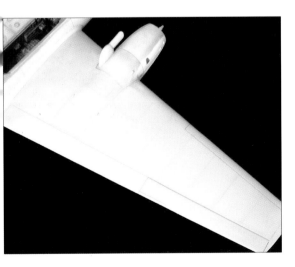

ABOVE The basic camouflage colours were sprayed on the airframe. This simple colour scheme comprised RLM 76 Light Blue lower surfaces and RLM 75 Grey Violet upper surfaces. Gunze paints were used, but their RLM 75 was lightened with RLM 76. The panel lines have not yet been shaded with a different colour. The effect seen here is as a result of a heavier coat of the basic colour being applied along panel lines.

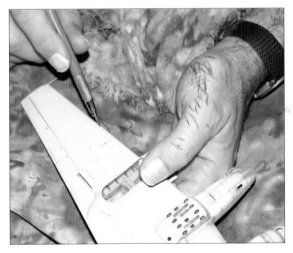

ABOVE A sharp 2B pencil was used to lightly draw along the panel lines on the lower surface. For pale colours, this method has a more subtle impact than a black wash.

ABOVE Before committing paint to plastic, the airbrush was tested on a scrap of paper to make sure the line is fine and consistent.

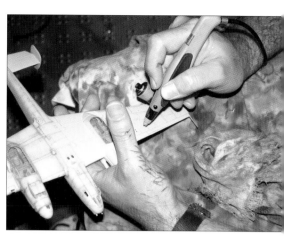

ABOVE The airbrush was used to trace over the pencil lines with a very thin mix of brown and black paint.

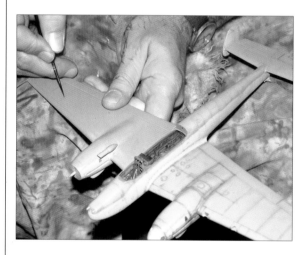

Above Panel lines on the upper surface were first painted with a wash of Tamiya Semi-Gloss Black, heavily thinned with water.

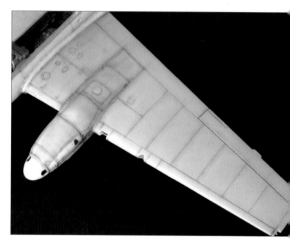

ABOVE Next, as with the lower surface, the panel lines were shaded very lightly with the airbrush.

Weathering panel lines on darker colours

Darker camouflage colours require a different treatment for panel lines.

The panel lines on the upper surfaces of this model were painted with a thin mixture of Tamiya X-18 Semi-Gloss Black and water. The semi-gloss paint seems to flow nicely into fine panel lines. It is important to note that this is not a sloppy wash – the heavily thinned paint is directed into the panel lines with a narrow brush and capillary action will tend to draw the watery mixture along the lines with minimal effort.

Once the initial highlighting has been completed, the panel lines are given the same treatment as the lower surfaces with the airbrushed brown/black mix.

Additional weathering

Exhaust stains were added by gradually building up layers of the brown/black mix on the wings.

Paint chipping on the wing walkways and around filler hatches was depicted with the point of a sharp silver artist's pencil.

The rusty exhausts were painted with, perhaps not surprisingly, Gunze Rust.

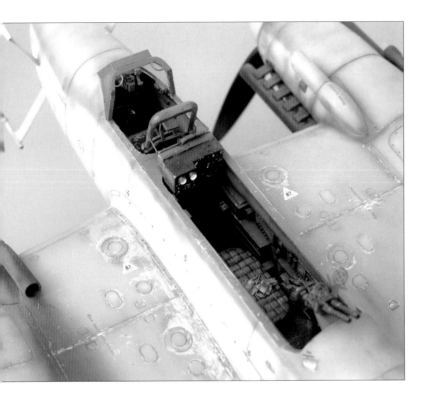

Additional weathering took the form of paint chipping on wing walkways using a silver pencil, rusty exhausts achieved with Gunze Rust, and airbrushed exhaust stains.

Finishing touches

Decals for this aircraft were sourced from AeroMaster sheet 48-322 – Nocturnal Birds of Prey Pt. III.

This aircraft was not fitted with the oblique-firing *Schrage Musik* cannon in the rear cockpit, so the canopy did not need the holes for the muzzles. Unfortunately, the holes are present in the optional open rear canopy. An alternate rear canopy section without the holes is also supplied with the kit, but this has the rear hatch moulded shut.

The hatch was carefully cut out of the clear plastic with a new scalpel blade. When this slightly frightening task was complete, the glasshouse canopy was masked with strips of Tamiya masking tape and the canopy frames were sprayed grey.

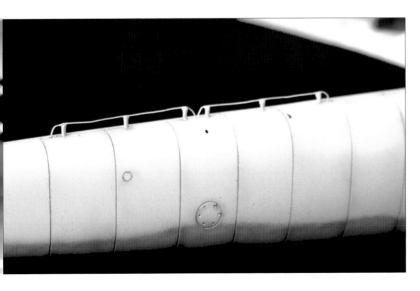

The clothesline antenna was replaced with picture wire. The outer sections of the antenna do not actually re-enter the fuselage as shown here. This was corrected later.

43

Once the masking tape was removed, rivet details were painted on the inner surfaces of the hatches with Flat Black paint. Details of the struts and hinges were added to the pilot's top hatch using plastic and stretched sprue.

The airframe was sprayed with Gunze acrylic Flat Clear. A ring and bead gunsight for the MG81Z twin rear machine gun was sourced from an Eduard photo-etched detail set. The completed gun was glued in the rear of the cockpit then the canopy was secured with G-S Hypo Cement, a strong, transparent jewellers' glue ideal for clear parts.

A length of smoke-coloured invisible mending thread was glued into a pre-drilled hole in the fin prior to painting. This was now attached to the mast and a lead-in wire fed into a tiny hole in the fuselage to complete the project.

This ProModeler Messerschmitt Bf 110G-4 delivers an impressive result with minimal aftermarket enhancement.

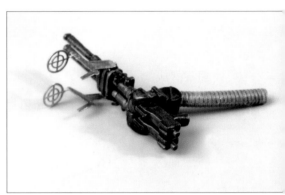

ABOVE The kit canopy was masked with strips of Tamiya masking tape and sprayed with Tamiya Dark Grey.

A handle was added to the pilot's top hatch from fine wire. Strut and hinge detail was also built for the hatch using plastic strip and stretched sprue. The opening mid-section was cut out of the solid plastic canopy. Rivet detail on the inside of the open hatches was painted onto the plastic with Flat Black and a fine brush.

ABOVE The MG81Z machine gun supplied with the kit is quite nicely detailed. This plastic part was supplemented with photo-etched brass gunsights from an Eduard detail set.

ABOVE Aerial wire has been added using smoke-coloured invisible mending thread.

ABOVE The front view of the Messerschmitt Bf 110G-4 is dominated by the radar array.

BELOW The larger trim tabs are obvious in this view. These were a characteristic of the larger rudder on the Bf 110G-4.

Master Project
Built, painted and weathered
by Brett Green

Improving the breed – correcting the Revell-Monogram Bf 110G

Although the ProModeler Bf 110G kit looks good straight from the box, it still suffers from the problem of undersized engine nacelles and spinners.

Correcting this problem is not easy. In addition to the engine nacelles themselves, any comprehensive solution needs to address the hump on each wing. This requires serious surgery to the kit.

For years, I wanted to build a ProModeler Bf 110G-4 with accurate cowlings, but the project always seemed beyond my modelling capabilities. I toyed with the idea of adapting Bf 110G conversion nacelles designed for the Fujimi Bf 110C kit. I even considered sacrificing the expensive Mauve kit by using the nacelles from that model on a ProModeler Bf 110G-4. However, the same issues always surfaced: the conversion nacelles were too narrow because they were designed to mate with Fujimi Bf 110C kit parts; and very significant scratch-building would be required behind the nacelle to adapt the new parts to the ProModeler wing.

Cutting Edge Modelworks fulfilled my wishes at the end of 2002 when they announced a Bf 110F/G correction set for the ProModeler and Revell kits.

As soon as I received my correction set from Cutting Edge I started work. Although construction usually commences with the cockpit, I decided to start with the wings and nacelles in this case.

The Cutting Edge Bf 110F/G correction set

Cutting Edge's Messerschmitt Bf 110F/G correction set comprises 22 parts perfectly cast in grey resin.

The set addresses the issues of the engine nacelles, the wing humps right back to the flaps, the exhausts, the spinners and the propeller blades. Two different styles of oil cooler are supplied. These represent standard and tropical housings. The cooling scoops on the upper wing bulge are also provided as separate parts.

Probably the most obvious problem with the ProModeler and Revell kits is the size of the spinners. The spinner from the real Bf 110G was the same factory

ProModeler's 1/48-scale Messerschmitt Bf 110G-4. The undersized engine nacelles, spinners and propellers have been replaced with resin items from Cutting Edge.

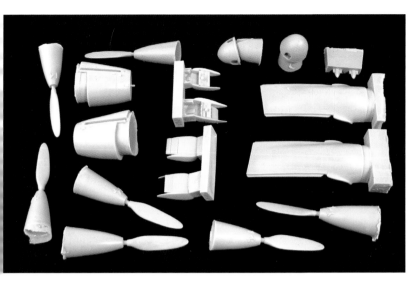

The resin components of Cutting Edge's 1/48-scale Messerschmitt Bf 110F/G correction set. This set includes two complete engine nacelles, spinners, propeller blades, replacement exhaust stubs and inserts for the upper wing.

item as the spinner for the Messerschmitt Bf 109F/G/K series. In 1/48 scale, the Revell spinner is almost 2mm smaller in diameter than the 17mm that it should be. Although 2mm might not sound like a large measurement, the ProModeler spinner does look puny compared to a full-sized Bf 109G spinner.

In addition to the size, the ProModeler part does not quite capture the side profile shape of the spinner, and also omits the thin circular cap covering the redundant hole for the cannon muzzle of the 109F/G/K series.

The single-piece Cutting Edge spinner is correctly sized and the shape looks much more accurate. The resin spinner, being a single part, has the pitch collars cast inside the spinner cap. The indentations need to be drilled out before placement of the propeller blades.

Engine nacelles

The Cutting Edge nacelles address all of the size and shape problems with the kit nacelles.

Each nacelle is supplied as a solid part. Panel line detail has been corrected, as has the position of the cut-out for the exhaust stacks.

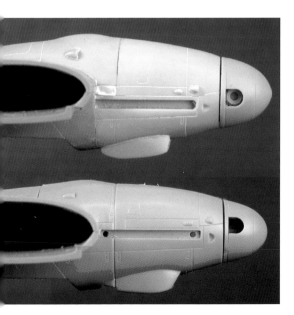

ABOVE This dramatic photograph demonstrates the need for a correction set! The resin replacement spinner is accurate in size and shape. It is 2mm bigger in diameter than its kit counterpart.

LEFT This illustrates the differences between the replacement resin nacelle from Cutting Edge (top) and the kit parts (below). The replacement parts are taller, giving a chunkier appearance to the nacelle area and the fairing on the upper wing. Also note the lower location of the exhaust cut-out.

The resin replacement nacelle is attached to a casting block. This block does not interfere with the fit of the part, and can stay in place as reinforcement during construction.

Wing hump insert

Cutting Edge addresses the incorrect wing hump with a resin insert for the wing behind the nacelle.

The hump is more accurate than the kit part, and the fairing over the magneto is much better defined than the same area on the ProModeler kit. The insert is cleverly engineered to ensure a snug fit with reinforcement ridges along the bottom of the part. The front of the hump rests on a ledge moulded as part of the kit wing.

Building the wing

First, the kit wings were prepared for the hump insert. This is by far the most intimidating aspect of the conversion, as a very significant chunk of the wing needs to be removed.

The cut takes place along the panel line surrounding the existing hump on the wing. This panel was traced repeatedly with a scriber, deepening the line to better define the area to be removed.

Next, I took a deep breath and started cutting the wing with a razor saw. I made sure that I cut inside the scored line, just in case the resin insert had shrunk. It is always easier to remove more plastic from a kit part than it is to fill, sand and smooth a big gap! As it turned out, test fitting showed that the inserts were an almost perfect match for the panel line, so the last microns were shaved up to the scored line with a sharp hobby knife.

Take care not to interfere with the lip that stretches back into the wing by around 1cm. This lip will support the front of the resin insert.

The wing inserts were now fitted to the upper wing halves. Gap-filling super glue was applied to the locating ridge along the rear edges of the insert, and to the lip near the front of the wing. Each insert was carefully positioned then secured with clamps until the super glue had set. The resulting joins were excellent. Some Mr Surfacer was brushed along the join lines to check for any problems before sanding and polishing.

The upper and lower wings were test fitted. The top of the wheel well interfered with the fit of the starboard wing. This was due to the resin insert being thicker

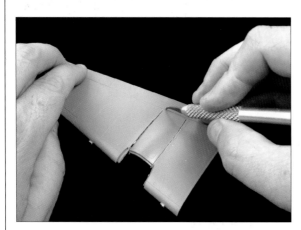

ABOVE The most challenging (and least forgiving) aspect of the correction is the removal of the entire panel incorporating the upper wing bulge from the ProModeler kit. The kit part was prepared by scribing the appropriate panel lines. This established a more positive guide for the razor saw.

ABOVE The golden rule of kit modification is 'cut less, then trim carefully'. The razor saw was used to make the cut just inside the scribed line. The resulting thin strip of excess plastic was cleaned up with a sharp scalpel blade after test-fitting the resin replacement bulge.

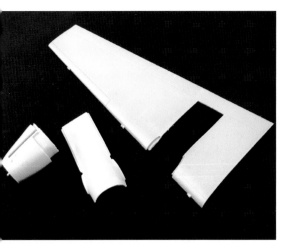

ABOVE The main wing components ready for assembly. Note that the lip on the inside of the kit wing near the leading edge has not been removed. This will provide support for the resin insert. The casting block on the back of the resin engine nacelle does not need to be removed. In fact, it adds rigidity to the join.

ABOVE Two clamps were used to hold the resin insert in place while the superglue set. The top of the wheel well bulge on the lower wing fouled against the resin insert. Plastic was filed away from the area indicated by the black diagonal shading in the picture.

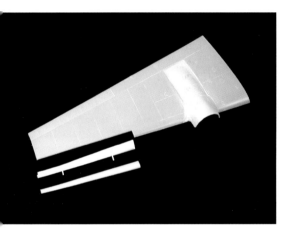

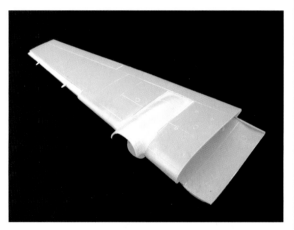

ABOVE The kit slats are moulded shut. These slats were removed with a new hobby knife. The resin insert and the slat are shown in this picture.

ABOVE The mounts that support the leading edge slats were installed before the upper and lower wings were joined, but the slats themselves were not added yet. In common with other delicate and small parts, these were left until after painting to avoid damage during construction.

than the kit part. The domes at the top of both wheel wells were sanded slightly until the top wings fitted properly.

I decided to install Cutting Edge control surfaces, including leading edge slats. The kit slats were removed by repeatedly scoring along the panel lines with a sharp hobby knife. The Cutting Edge slats include a resin mounting strip that slots into the gap left in the wing leading edge. The two mounts for the extended slats are cast onto this base. The resin of the base needed to be thinned toward the outside of the part, but these resin slats were much easier and faster to prepare and install than the scratch-built items created for the Bf 110E described earlier in this book!

The slat mount was glued to the upper wing, holes were drilled for the drop tanks and the wing halves were finally joined.

The fit of the resin nacelle to the kit wing was generally good except for the join at the outboard rear nacelle on each side. This area required significant filler and sanding to smooth the join.

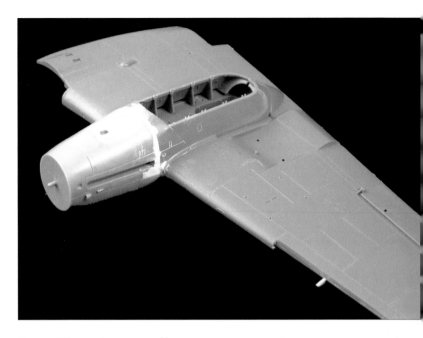

Installing the nacelles

The lower rear of the kit nacelle parts incorporating the main wheel bay (part numbers 11, 12, 13 and 14) was cut off each main nacelle halves.

This cut is not along a panel line so careful planning was required. With the nacelle removed, the remaining wheel well sections were glued onto the lower wing.

Checking the fit of the resin nacelle against the face of the wing and the wheel well showed that I had cut off too much plastic from each outboard nacelle half. This resulted in a large, uniform gap on the outboard side of each nacelle. I glued the resin nacelles to the wing then filled the gaps with Milliput putty on the starboard side, and with a sliver of plastic on the port side.

After the nacelle was glued in place, there was also a small rectangular gap above and near the rear of each exhaust cut-out. These gaps were filled with chunks of scrap white Plasticard, then sliced flat and sanded.

Dressing up the cockpit

ProModeler's cockpit is very respectable straight from the box, but I wanted to really dress up this highly exposed area of the kit.

Aires offer several update sets for the Revell-Monogram family of Bf 110Gs including a cockpit comprising 22 resin parts, 28 photo-etched parts and a printed acetate sheet. The set is beautifully detailed.

However, initial test fitting against the kit fuselage indicated that the resin fuselage sidewalls, rear bulkhead and floor (in other words, all the major cockpit parts) were far too large. The fuselage sidewalls were cut shorter and trimmed along the bottom to improve the fit. The rear bulkhead was similarly trimmed. The cockpit floor was a different matter. It was not only too long but too thick, having the potential to seriously interfere with the fit of the wing. Rather than spend a few hours cloaked in resin dust while this part was sanded down to wafer thinness, I decided to use the kit floor, which was pretty well detailed anyway.

The radio was also too wide and too deep. Trimming the edges would have destroyed the relative proportions of the radio boxes, so I cut the top off the main radio and used the kit part instead.

The back of the resin sidewalls were sanded until translucent, then glued to the kit fuselage halves.

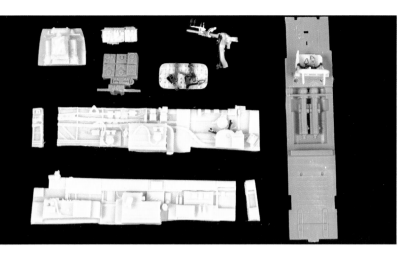

Some of the Aires resin parts used to detail the cockpit area. The sidewalls, rear bulkhead and floor parts were all too big. Some parts were virtually unusable, such as the radio and the floor. These were simply replaced with their corresponding kit parts, while the sidewalls were shortened in length (as illustrated here) and further trimmed along the bottom.

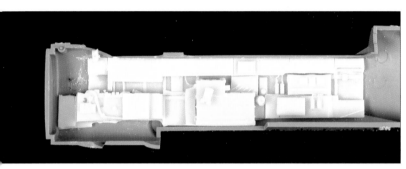

The resin sidewalls were sanded paper-thin before being glued to the kit fuselage. This picture shows that the resin parts are translucent in places.

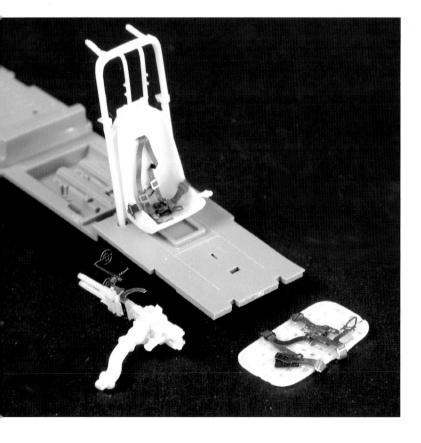

Notwithstanding the ill-fitting main components, the detail parts represented a big improvement on the kit parts. The MG81Z machine gun, the 'woven' rear seat and the instrument panel were especially noteworthy.

Despite the frustration of the oversized resin main parts, the smaller details were outstanding. Items such as the MG81Z machine gun, the woven rear seat, instrument panel and pilot's rollover cage represented a big improvement over the kit parts. The photo-etched harness was attached to the pilot's seat, which, in turn, was glued to the mount and the roll bar. The completed seat assembly was glued onto the plastic kit floor. Two sets of lap harnesses were also added to the rear seat – the crewmembers in the rear sat back to back on the single seat.

Painting the cockpit

Detail parts were tacked to a small note pad in preparation for painting. I find this is helpful to avoid fingerprints and to keep track of where the parts are.

The cockpit then received a thorough coat of flat black. This black paint acts as a 'shadow coat', and will show through the lighter top colour in undercuts and recesses as darker areas. Next, Tamiya XF-63 German Grey was sprayed at a constant downward angle to retain some of the black in naturally shaded areas.

RIGHT Small detail parts were tacked to a small note pad so that they would not be lost during painting.

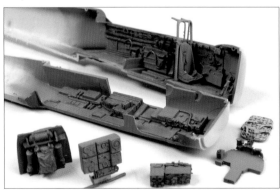

ABOVE All cockpit parts were first sprayed flat black. This black paint acts as a 'shadow coat'. Next, the components receive a coat of dark grey, sprayed at a constant downward angle in order to retain some of the black in natural shadow areas.

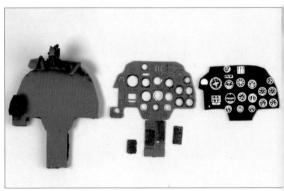

ABOVE The instrument panel comprises a resin base with a photo-etched metal face sandwiching an acetate sheet with printed instruments. After receiving a basic coat of dark grey, instrument bezels were picked out in black, red, yellow and blue.

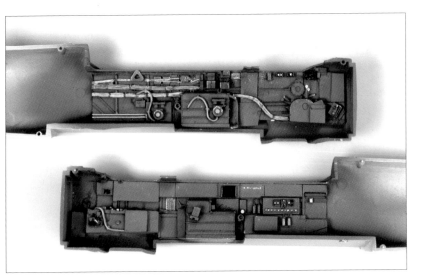

LEFT Electrical cables, throttle knobs, oxygen hoses and other details on the cockpit sidewalls were brush-painted using Tamiya acrylics.

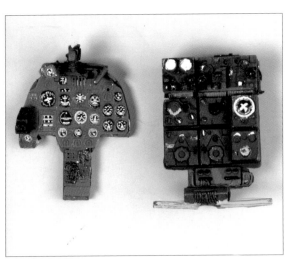

ABOVE The completed instrument panel and kit radio.

ABOVE The woven rear seat, rear bulkhead and MG81Z machine gun. The seat and ammunition bags received a wash of thinned Winsor and Newton Burnt Umber oil paint to highlight the fabric textures of these parts.

Following the application of the basic grey, structural details such as cabling, hoses, throttles and knobs were brush-painted using Tamiya acrylics.

The instrument panel comprised a printed acetate sheet sandwiched between a resin base (which was cast with raised detail including the gunsight) and a brass panel. The bezels were painted by poking a fine brush loaded with paint through the back of the instrument holes in the panel. This seems to produce a fairly reliable, fine outline to the instrument hole in whatever colour is required. Most of the bezels on the Bf 110G cockpit were black, but some were also painted yellow and blue.

With the top panel finished and the acetate instruments backed with white paint, the three pieces were joined with G-S Hypo Cement, applied sparingly.

The rear seat and ammunition bags received a wash of thinned Winsor and Newton Burnt Umber oil paint to highlight the fabric texture of these parts.

Thanks to the hours of preparation and test fitting, the cockpit components fitted without problems between the fuselage halves.

RIGHT AND BELOW RIGHT The cockpit components were fitted in preparation for the joining of the fuselage halves.

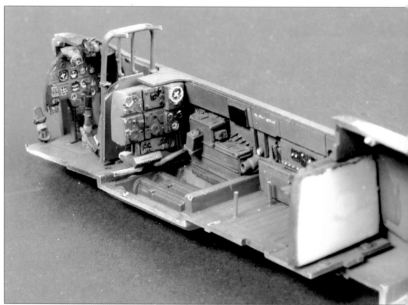

Airframe construction

The remaining construction was completed surprisingly quickly.

The main problem area was the fit at the lower wing and fuselage joins. The kit has a curious method of joining the lower wings with the fuselage. Instead of a conventional full-span lower wing, or separate wings with locating tabs at the wing roots, Revell has supplied one lower wing half that extends all the way across the bottom of the fuselage and another which butts up against this part.

The starboard wing (with the lower fuselage section incorporated) was first glued onto the fuselage. When the starboard wing was set, the port wing was tacked in place with a few spots of super glue, and then Tamiya Extra Thin Liquid Glue was applied with a fine brush along all the join lines to ensure a strong bond. The dihedral looked fractionally understated once the wings were actually in place but the parts breakdown leaves very little margin for adjustment.

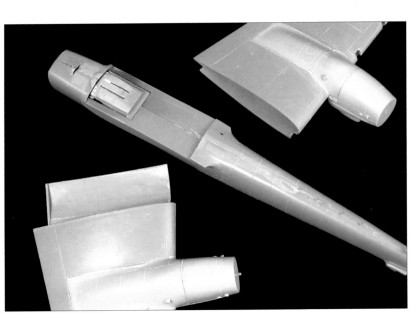

The main kit components ready to assemble. Note the unusual join between the lower wing parts.

LEFT The lower wing join resulted in a step that required sanding. The fit was also poor at the leading and trailing edges of the lower wing. Putty can be seen in these areas.

BELOW LEFT In contrast to the lower wing join, the fit at the upper wing roots was excellent.

BELOW RIGHT The oft-discussed mould flaw on the upper fuselage of the ProModeler kit was quickly eliminated with a little Liquid Paper (used as filler) and a coat of Gunze Mr Surfacer followed by light sanding.

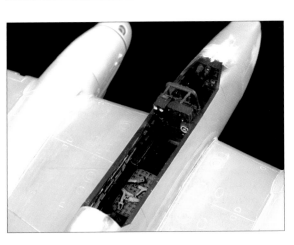

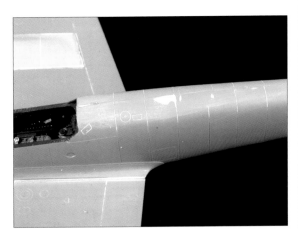

ABOVE The angle of the starboard engine supercharger intake is wrong. The kit parts were first joined.

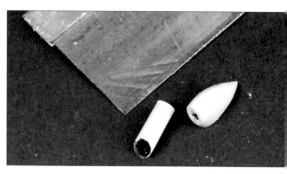

ABOVE The straight pipe was then cut off using a razor saw.

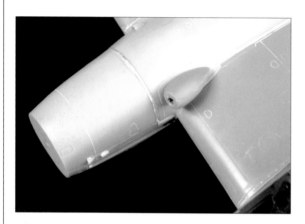

ABOVE The bulbous base was glued to the rear of the engine nacelle.

ABOVE The intake pipe was then glued to the base at the correct angle.

The resulting join still required some extra work. There was a noticeable step at the lower wing join and slight gaps where the front and back of the wing met the fuselage. The gaps were filled using Liquid Paper straight from the bottle, even using the brush supplied in the cap. While the Liquid Paper was out, I also filled the mould flaw on the top of the fuselage. The Liquid Paper dried fast and was sanded first with Tamiya 400 grit abrasive paper, followed by 1,000-grit paper.

A line of Gunze Mr Surfacer 500 was brush-painted along the wing. The areas previously filled with Liquid Paper also received a coat. The wing join was then smoothed with a sanding stick before the remaining spots of Mr Surfacer were sanded back.

Mr Surfacer is a great product for finishing models. However, it is best gently dry-sanded when it is painted on thick, otherwise the plastic skin will tend to peel off. I usually start with a small section of new 400-grit sandpaper, rubbing in gentle, slow circles until I can see sections of plastic showing through. This is followed with a dry-sanding with 1,000-grit paper. When the 1,000-grit paper gets worn, only then will I dampen it and finish with a quick wet sand. The repaired areas are then polished with a nail buffer or a specialist hobby polishing stick.

The angle of the starboard engine supercharger intake was corrected and glued onto the engine nacelle.

Tail surfaces

Cutting Edge resin control surfaces were used for the elevators and rudders. These are nicely detailed parts with deflected trim tabs and finely rendered actuators. The plastic elevators and rudders were cut from the kit parts and the joining edge of

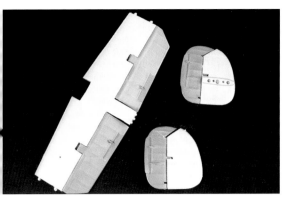

ABOVE Cutting Edge resin control surfaces were used to deflect the elevators and rudders. Note that these are the larger rudders found on most Messerschmitt Bf 110G-4s.

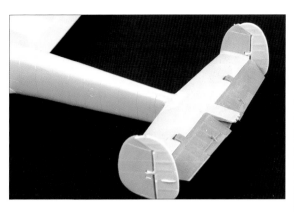

ABOVE The tailplanes in place. At this stage I had discovered my error and replaced the rudders with the earlier, small version.

ABOVE My second major error was the installation of the wrong nose. My subject aircraft was fitted with the earlier, four-machine-gun nose. The only option was to cut off the nose and replace it with the resin kit part. I started with a razor saw, removing the nose cap.

ABOVE The solid resin nose had a substantial casting plug at its rear. Instead of grinding this off I decided it would be easier to remove the forward fuselage bulkhead. A Dremel motor tool fitted with a cutting disc was used to slice the bulkhead into sections.

the horizontal stabilizer was thinned in preparation for the elevators. The resin parts were glued in place using super glue and the tail surfaces attached to the model.

Intermission

Construction was powering along and I started to think about painting and markings.

I had my subject chosen – a Bf 110G-4 fitted with early FuG 202 Lichtenstein radar. There are two excellent photos of this aircraft in Monogram Close Up 18: *Bf 110G* (now sadly out of print). To my dawning horror, I realised that I had glued on the wrong nose and the wrong rudders! This particular aircraft was fitted with the machine-gun nose and the early-style narrow rudders.

There was no choice other than to cut off these parts and substitute the correct components.

The rudders did not present a problem. They snapped off with the application of minimal force. The nose was not so easy. I had thoroughly secured this part with liquid glue and I risked splitting the fuselage if I tried to snap it off.

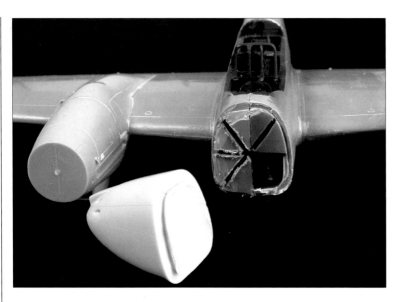

I therefore took to the forward fuselage with a razor saw. Once the nose cap was removed and the excess plastic was cleaned up with a hobby knife, I was presented with the protruding forward fuselage bulkhead.

The resin nose from the Revell Bf 110G-2 boxing was slated for this area, and that part featured a casting block at the back. I decided I would be easier to remove the plastic bulkhead from the kit fuselage than to remove the casting block.

The Dremel motor tool was fitted with a cutting wheel and set to a low speed. The bulkhead was sliced into sections in seconds. These sections were simply snapped off and the new opening at the front of the fuselage was trimmed to a neat finish.

Fortunately, the resin nose was a near-perfect fit for the forward fuselage with only minimal filling required.

Radar

Cutting Edge rescued me from the task of scratch-building the early radar with their FuG 202 Lichtenstein radar set. This comprises 16 sets of tiny brass dipoles plus one mount and four radar posts in resin.

Although the resin parts were connected to their blocks with thin resin, extreme care was required during their removal as the arms for the radar posts are extremely delicate. After the four posts were removed from their casting blocks the brass dipoles were test fitted. These dipoles were small, but they were still too long. Without trimming they would have overlapped in the middle. Each dipole was cut approximately 1mm shorter. The dipoles were now fitted to the posts with super glue.

The main mount is designed to simply glue to the nose of the model. I decided to reinforce that important join with a length of brass wire. The aircraft nose and the mount were both drilled out, and the brass wire was installed in the mount.

Patience, time and care was the most effective formula for aligning and securing the radar posts on the main mount.

Although the brass dipoles are certainly fine, I think they still look too chunky. If I ever build another early Lichtenstein array, I will probably use stretched sprue for the radar dipoles.

Canopy

The rear portions of both rear canopy parts, with and without holes for the *Schrage Musik* cannon (kit part numbers 94 and 101), were cut off with a razor saw. The back part of the canopy without the holes was mated to the front half of the canopy with the open hatch. All clear parts then received a bath in Future floor wax and set aside to dry for several hours.

Black Magic self-adhesive masks were used to mask the canopy. The Black Magic masks resulted in a very fast and precise result for an otherwise time consuming and tedious job.

All the canopy components were backed with masking tape to avoid over spray on the back of the parts.

The canopy parts were first sprayed with Tamiya XF-63 Dark Grey to represent the interior colour, then Polly Scale acrylic RLM 74 as the top camouflage colour.

ABOVE The FuG 202 Lichtenstein radar was made up of resin mounts and tiny brass dipoles. First, the resin parts were very carefully removed from their blocks using a razor saw and a sharp knife.

ABOVE Next, the vertical dipoles were test-fitted and cut shorter before being secured to the small mounts with super glue. The centre rear of the main mount was drilled out and fitted with a short length of brass wire to establish a solid join at the aircraft nose.

ABOVE The nose was also drilled out to accept the wire pin. The resin mount was test-fitted to confirm correct alignment.

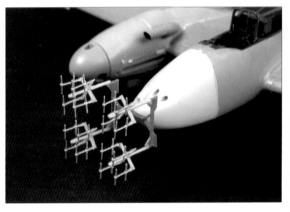

ABOVE Patience, time and care is the most effective formula for the final alignment and securing of the radar posts on the main mount.

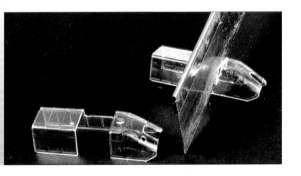

ABOVE I wanted to show off the rear cockpit detail, but the kit part without the holes for the *Schrage Musik* cannon does not offer the option of an opening rear canopy. I cut off the non-*Schrage Musik* canopy section using a razor saw, and then did the same with the *Schrage Musik* canopy.

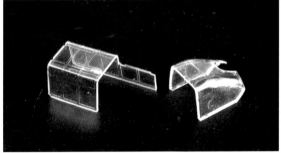

ABOVE The rearmost canopy section without the cannon holes was mated with the open mid-canopy section. When the components were separated, all the clear parts received a bath in Future floor polish for a sparkling shine.

ABOVE The canopy parts were masked with Black Magic self-adhesive vinyl masks. These are a handy timesaving accessory for a complex masking task. The clear parts were backed with masking tape to avoid overspray on the back of the parts, and to better judge the opacity of the paint coat.

ABOVE The canopy parts were first sprayed with dark grey to depict the colour of the interior framework, then with RLM 74 Grey as the top camouflage colour.

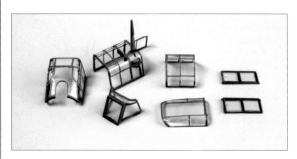

ABOVE Removal of the masks shows crisp and consistent framework.

ABOVE The Cutting Edge correction set includes lengthened exhaust stubs to compensate for the lower position of the exhaust cut-outs on the replacement nacelles. The ends of the kit flame dampers were hollowed out using a Dremel motor tool, and glued to the resin stubs

Detail parts

In preparation for painting and final assembly, the various detail parts were built and painted:

8-amp fuse wire was used to represent hydraulic lines on the main undercarriage legs.

- Each flame damper exhaust was drilled out at the end and fitted to the new resin stacks.
- The solid resin propeller spinners were painted overall white. The spinner cap was masked with strips of tape and the next colour, Polly Scale RLM 76 Light Blue, was applied. A disc was cut out of a self-adhesive Post-It Note and, after the masking tape was removed, this was lined up as a mask to spray a circle of RLM 76 at the tip of the spinner. A black wash was applied to the propeller hub and other undercut areas inside the spinner before the propeller blades were fitted. The locating holes are very shallow. In retrospect I should have reinforced this join with wire.
- The 'clothes rail' antenna under the fuselage was fabricated from copper wire
- The undercarriage legs in the kit lean too far forward without modification I shortened the retraction struts (kit part 58 x 2) by approximately 2mm This brought the gear legs back a few degrees. Soft fuse wire was also run down the side of each main gear leg to depict hydraulic lines.
- The resin slats were glued to the front of the wings

The model was now ready for paint.

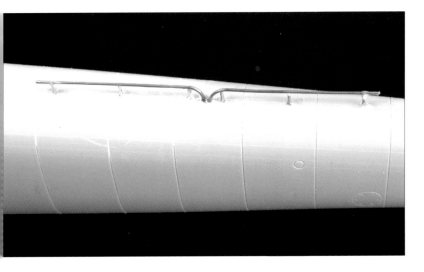

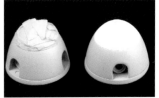

ABOVE The resin spinners were first painted white, then carefully masked and sprayed with RLM 76 Light Blue. Later, the tip of the spinner was masked with a small circle cut from a Post-It Note using a steel punch, and sprayed with RLM 76, resulting in a white band around the spinner.

ABOVE LEFT The 'clothes rail' antenna was scratch-built from copper wire, replacing the plastic masts broken off during construction.

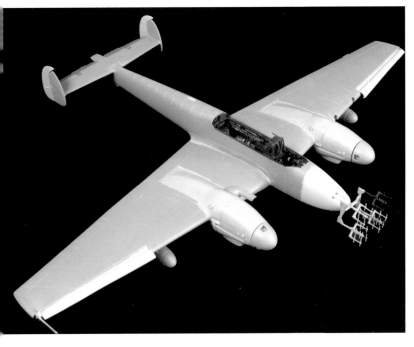

LEFT The model ready for paint.

Painting and Markings

Camouflage scheme

Messerschmitt Bf 110G-4 2Z+OP wore an unusual camouflage scheme for a night fighter. It featured RLM 74 Grey Green and RLM 75 Grey Violet upper surfaces with a very low demarcation on the fuselage. The nose was mottled with RLM 76 Light Blue. The lower starboard wing and drop tank were also painted black as an identification aid to German Flak gunners.

This aircraft landed accidentally in Switzerland on 15 March 1944.

Painting a pre-shaded camouflage finish

This model was painted by means of a technique called pre-shading. Under this method, panel lines are painted a dark colour before camouflage colours are painted over the top. The pre-shaded panel lines do not have to be terribly precise. Overspray can be tidied up later.

Wheel wells, intakes and the canopy were masked before the starboard lower wing received its 'scale black' coat. This was the same mix of Tamiya XF-1 Black

ABOVE Panel lines were pre-shaded in black. This technique does not require great precision, as this photo clearly demonstrates!

ABOVE The lower starboard wing was painted an overall coat of Tamiya Flat Black mixed 50/50 with Tamiya Red Brown. This 'scale black' mix permits weathering along panel lines in 100 per cent black, and looks quite convincing.

ABOVE The camouflage colours were used to fill in the spaces between the pre-shaded panel lines. Once this task was completed, the model received misted coats of the camouflage colours to tone down the dark panel lines until the desired effect was obtained.

ABOVE The camouflage pattern has been sprayed entirely freehand using an Aztek A470 airbrush fitted with the tan-coloured *Fine* nozzle. The interesting mottling on the nose is obvious in this view. The sooty base coat of the exhaust stain has already been applied to one wing.

and XF-64 Red Brown that was used as the overall colour on the Bf 110E earlier in this book.

While the airbrush was loaded with this colour, the panel lines and crevices on the lower surface were outlined. Upper surface panel lines received the same treatment using black paint.

Next, the Aztek A470 airbrush was loaded with Polly Scale acrylic RLM 76 Light Blue and the spaces between the dark panel lines were filled in. Once this was finished, the bottom of the port wing, tailplanes and fuselage received several misted coats of RLM 76 until the dark shaded lines were almost invisible.

This process was repeated on the upper surfaces with the first camouflage colour, Polly Scale RLM 75 Grey Violet. The disruptive RLM 74 Grey Green pattern was sprayed freehand. The reference photos in the Monogram Close Up book were used wherever possible, and the AeroMaster instructions were adopted as a guide for the pattern on the top of the wings.

ABOVE All the detail parts were built and painted as separate components, to be assembled after the main airframe had been painted.

ABOVE Various aerials and the ladder were put in place on the lower fuselage.

ABOVE The dark pre-shading of panel lines faintly shows through the camouflage colours. The panel lines have also been highlighted with a very thin wash of semi-gloss black acrylic paint. The exhaust stains have been detailed with a pale chalky grey along the centre of the sooty black.

ABOVE The resin control surfaces include deflected trim tabs and nicely detailed actuators. Rear navigation lights were each painted white, then received a spot of Tamiya Clear Red, Smoke and Gunze Clear Green to represent the colours of the bulbs.

RLM 76 Light Blue was loaded again to apply the pale mottle to the nose.

Panel lines on the lower surface and nose were traced with a sharp 2B pencil. In fact, the panel lines on the resin nose were so fine that I had to apply masking tape as a guide to ensure the pencil lines were straight. A thin black acrylic wash was applied to the structural features on the upper surface. Minor chipping of wing walks was added with a sharp silver artists' pencil.

A coat of Polly Scale Gloss Clear was sprayed before decal from AeroMaster sheet 48-321, Nocturnal Birds of Prey Part II. The decals behaved perfectly, and the airframe received a final coat of Polly Scale Flat Clear before final assembly.

Finishing touches

The detail parts that were assembled and painted earlier were now fitted to the model.

All that remained were a few finishing touches. Aerial wire was fitted using invisible mending thread, clear parts were installed including the landing light and the wing formation lights, and the rear formation lights were painted white then received a coat of Tamiya Clear Red for the port side and Gunze Clear Green for the starboard. A light wash of black was placed over these rear formation lights to highlight the outlines.

ABOVE Segmented grey camouflage with a low fuselage demarcation line was very unusual for a Bf 110G-4 of this period.

BELOW This aircraft landed accidentally in Switzerland on 15 March 1944.

ABOVE Compass swings were frequently seen on German airfields during World War II.

BELOW The 1/48-scale compass swing and accessories are from Verlinden Productions.

Bringing your Bf 110 to life – accessorising your model with a base and figures

A convincing base can be a valuable accessory for your model aircraft. A realistic and relevant base can add interest and context, whether you plan to display or photograph your model.

There are many options for aircraft model bases available today, with after market companies offering a choice of products in resin, vacform plastic ceramic and polystyrene. Specific subjects and theatres are covered, including PSP metal airfields, aircraft carrier decks, Luftwaffe hardstands and many more

Because I photograph my models, I like my bases to be large and versatile They need to be large for the edges of the base to stay out of the shot even under models with big wingspans; and they need to be versatile enough to provide different 'views' in order to minimize the number of bases in my collection.

The use of the compass swing displays the Bf 110-G4 model at an interesting and unusual angle.

I also hold a stock of generic Luftwaffe and Allied figures that are used in photographs from time to time.

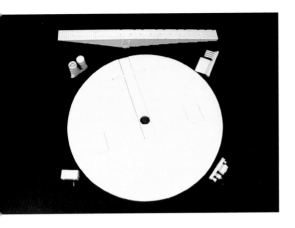

ABOVE Verlinden's Luftwaffe compass swing makes an eye-catching accessory for a display stand. It comprises two large parts in resin plus some handy airfield accessories.

ABOVE Architectual foam board was used as the material for the base. An Olfa compass cutter was used to remove a circle from this board.

Composing a Luftwaffe compass platform setting

Verlinden's re-released 1/48-scale Luftwaffe compass swing seemed to be an excellent opportunity to build a new airfield base.

Verlinden's compass swing represents a wooden structure that was used to service and check aircraft and their armament. The wooden platform sat over a pit with a mechanism that permitted it to swing. A concrete ring surrounded most of these platforms. The entire assembly was sometimes installed on a grass airstrip, and sometimes on sealed airfield surfaces.

My plan was to install the compass platform off-centre in a large base board, then surround the platform with a section of concrete airfield, and add a border of dirt and grass around one side and a strip at the rear. This arrangement would permit me to photograph a model on the compass swing on one side of the base; or shoot an aircraft on concrete tarmac on the other side.

I bought a sheet of architectural foamboard and cut a hole with an Olfa compass cutter in preparation of the installation of the round platform. By sheer luck, the depth of the foamboard matched the depth of the platform.

The resin components of Verlinden's compass swing were assembled in minutes. It was now time to paint.

Five steps to painting timber airfield elements

I follow five basic steps when painting timber airfield elements:

Base coat

Timber does not remain brown for long once it is exposed to the elements. It fades to a grubby grey shade. The entire surface is therefore primed in a pale grey-buff colour. I used a mix of 50 per cent Tamiya acrylic XF-19 Sky Grey and 50 per cent XF-57 Buff.

Non-timber features

Large, non-timber features are now painted. The sides of the ramp girder and the doors were painted Tamiya XF-63 German Grey.

Airbrushed weathering

The airbrush was used to add random patches and stains to the overall platform. I started with a thin mix of Tamiya XF-52 Earth Brown and a few drops of Dark Grey. This was followed by another pass with a darker grey mix. Be careful not to overdo this stage! Other features

The compass swing has received its base coat and the first weathering coat of dirty brown, randomly airbrushed.

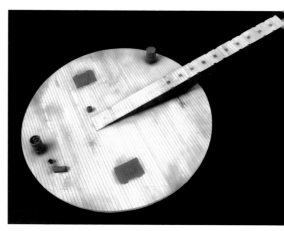

ABOVE The sides of the rail and other elements have been picked out in dark colours. The second airbrushed weathering coat, dark grey, has been applied.

ABOVE Here is the platform after a wash of Winsor and Newton Raw Umber oil paint, followed by detailing of selected individual planks and application of oil stains.

were also detailed with the airbrush. The dark sides of the ramp were streaked with black.

Oil wash

The entire platform received a generous wash of Winsor and Newton Raw Umber oil paint thinned in turpentine. The platform was now set aside until dry. This is likely to take a few hours in a hot environment – longer if it is cool.

Detail weathering and painting

Individual planks were picked out in different shades of tan, dark yellow, pink and grey. Oil stains were added using thinned black acrylic paint. Smaller parts were also painted in detail at this stage.

Finishing the base

The foamboard base was sprayed in a mottled finish of XF-57 Buff and XF-19 Sky Grey over the base grey colour. The board was marked with a grid of 6in. squares representing expansion strips. These lines were heavily overdrawn with a 2B pencil, slightly recessing the expansion strips in the soft foamboard.

ABOVE The cardboard-faced foam board has been drawn on with a random mottle of grey and buff. Expansion strips and cracks have been painted using a sharp 2B pencil.

ABOVE The resin compass swing was tested for fit.

Tools and materials for groundwork are assembled. The base for the groundwork is a Heki, a brown adhesive. This is a messy business and is best completed outdoors.

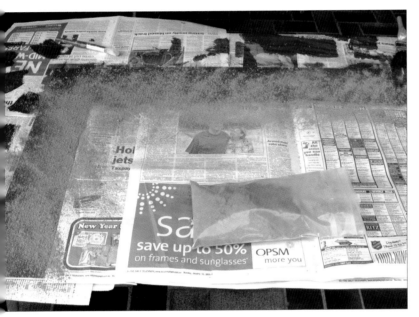

The 'concrete' sections of the airfield are masked with sheets of newspaper before the adhesive is brushed on and flattened down. Brown 'dirt' groundwork and static grass are scattered on to the brown glue. The excess is blown off the base, and the remaining material is sprayed with water to seal the groundwork in place.

The groundwork dries to give a parched and dusty finish.

Here is a 1/48-scale crewmembers viewpoint, with a photographic background behind the base.

I use a model railway groundwork adhesive called Heki. This is brown in colour and thick in texture. The real advantage of this glue is that total coverage is not required – the brown adhesive looks like muddy earth.

The next stage of construction is messy, and should definitely be undertaken outside.

The concrete sections of the airfield were masked with sheets of newspaper before the adhesive was brushed on. The first pass with the brush left many bubbles and lumps, so I spent a few minutes smoothing out the finish.

TUFT is a landscaping material available in many shades: dirt, earth, mud, sand and grass. A dry earth mix was generously sprinkled on the adhesive, followed by a further random coverage of static grass. The excess dirt and grass was blown off the board before the surface was sprayed with a misting of water from a domestic spray bottle. This is an important step as it cements the TUFT groundwork in place.

Once the newspaper mask has been removed and the groundwork has set to its parched and dusty finish, any excess material was bumped off the board and the compass swing was fitted underneath.

Making a base does not require a big investment in time or money. It is certainly an effective way to personalize your model.

Photographic background

Once the base is finished, it is helpful to have a relevant and realistic backdrop against which to display it. This is especially important if you are planning to photograph your models in this setting.

Several options are available for backgrounds:

- Plain blue cardboard can be used to represent a cloudless sky
- Model railway scenic backgrounds are available with a wide variety of scenes.
- Photographs of real scenery can be enlarged

The background to these models is a photograph taken by George Pfromm of an old German airfield in Belgium. The photo was enlarged to poster size and glued to a piece of architectural foamboard. This ensures that the photo stays flat, and makes storage easier.

Figures

Figures are a useful addition to your base. Figures provide scale – observers can see how big the real aircraft was with a pilot standing alongside. They also help identify the era, and carefully placed figures can suggest a story.

1/48-scale figures are more common now than they used to be. I saw Andrea's Luftwaffe fighter figures and decided that they would look right at home with my Messerschmitt Bf 110E night fighter.

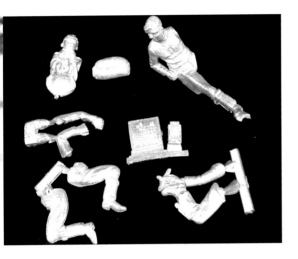

ABOVE Andrea's white metal figures are provided in components.

ABOVE The figures were painted and primed. The standing figure is from Airwaves. He is not as well-detailed or cast as the two seated Andrea figures.

ABOVE Painting is well under way. I generally brush-paint demarcation lines then spray the rest of the figures.

ABOVE The figures are painted, washed and have details picked out – ready to place with an aircraft.

Andrea's figures are supplied in white metal but they are as nicely detailed as many resin or plastic releases. When using white metal figures, however, it is always a good idea to prepare the surface with a metal primer. This will help the paint stick, and protect the finished piece from bumps and scratches.

My approach to painting 1/48-scale figures might be termed impressionistic rather than realistic – I want to create the overall impression of the figure, as the figures will not be the focus of the setting.

Once the figures were primed, I brush-painted demarcation lines in the appropriate colours – i.e., where the neck meets the collar, the boots meet the trousers etc. I then used the airbrush to finish painting the larger areas such as the uniforms, boots and heads.

High spots such as the crease in uniforms, forehead, bridge of the nose and ears were painted in a lighter shade with a fine brush.

The figures received a wash of thinned Winsor and Newton Raw Umber oil paint on the uniform and boots, and Winsor and Newton Burnt Sienna on the faces. More detail was brush painted after the wash had dried.

This technique is fairly fast and quite adequate for figures that are destined to live in the shadow of a model aeroplane!

Messerschmitt Bf 110 gallery

Mauve 1/48-scale Messerschmitt Bf 110G-4
Model by Chris Wauchop

Mauve is a Japanese model company that released a limited-edition 1/48-scale Messerschmitt Bf 110G-4 kit in 1992. This kit was based on the Fujimi BF 110C/D kit, with additional high quality plastic sprues with new engine nacelles, radar mounts, nose, rudders and rear canopy section. The model also featured a large number of white metal detail parts and a photo-etched fret, mainly destined for the cockpit, and fine brass rod and tube for the radar arrays. A nice decal sheet with three marking options was also provided.

Although the kit corrected several of the Fujimi kit's worst problem areas by detailing the cockpit and replacing the awful spinners, many other issues remained unaddressed. The Fujimi wheel wells, small rear wheel, drop tanks and their racks were all used on this expensive model.

However, the Mauve kit is really quite accurate. The profile of the nacelles and spinners is good, although the nacelles are slightly narrow – a legacy of the narrower Bf 110C/D nacelle mount.

Revell-Monogram Messerschmitt Bf 110F-2
Model by Chris Wauchop

This Revell-Monogram kit was labeled as a Messerschmitt Bf 110G-2, but the under-wing pitot tube actually identifies this aircraft as a Bf 110F-2.

The subject aircraft featured a ventral gun pack, with either one or two 20mm cannon. This installation prompted the removal of the 30mm cannon in the upper nose. Although the MK108 was a heavy-hitting weapon, the 20mm cannon had a larger capacity for ammunition and therefore extended the combat capability of the aircraft.

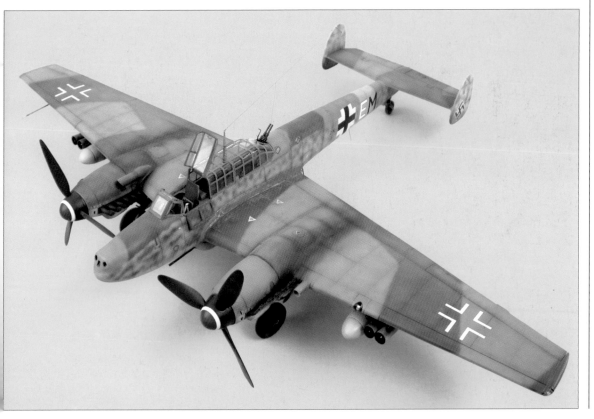

BELOW The small drop tanks and long mounts are obvious in this view.

Arba 1/48-scale Messerschmitt Bf 110G-4 Conversion
Model by Brett Green

Long before the Mauve or Revell-Monogram Bf 110G-4 kits were available, Arba released a resin conversion based on Fujimi's 1/48-scale Bf 110C/D kit.

Solid resin nacelles, spinners, nose and inserts for the upper wing humps were supplemented with white metal rudders and radar. These parts were crude by today's standards. The solid resin nacelles featured shallow, blank faces for the oil coolers. All the white metal parts were pitted and needed plenty of preparation. A vacform canopy was supplied, but the surface had a pebbly texture. In common with the later Mauve kit, many of the Fujimi kit shortcomings were ignored.

However, the model looks like a Bf 110G-4 when the conversion pieces are added.

I detailed the cockpit with Eduard's first photo-etched set for the Fujimi kit, No. 48-056, and with many scratch-built and scavenged items. The radar was replaced with the FuG 218 Neptun radar in Dragon's 1/48-scale Horten Ho 229 night fighter kit.

Further Reading, Media and Websites

Further reading

Aders, *History of the German Night Fighter Force: 1917–1945*, (Jane's, London, 1979)

Anderton and Watanabe, *Interceptor vs. Heavy Bomber*, (Aggressors series, No. 3; Howell Press, 1991)

Bentley et al., *Fighters of World War Two, Vol. 1*, (Aircraft Archive series, Motorbooks International, 1988)

Birkholz (ed.), *Foto-Archiv: Band 7*, (Jet & Prop Foto-Archiv series, No. 7; VDM Heinz Nickel, 1997)

Brown, *Wings of the Luftwaffe*, (Doubleday, New York, 1978)

Cohausz, *Cockpits deutscher Flugzeug: Historische Instrumentierungen von 1911–1970*, (Aviatic Verlag, 2000)

Cuny, *La Chasse de Nuit Allemande 1939–1945*, (E.P.A., 1980)

Donald (ed.), *Warplanes of the Luftwaffe*, (Aerospace, 1994)

Weal, J., 'Luftwaffe Nachtflieger, Part 2', In *Wings of Fame*, Volume 15 (Aerospace, 1999)

Ebert, Kaiser and Peters, *Willy Messerschmitt – Pioneer of Aviation Design*, (The History of German Aviation series, No. 3; Schiffer, New York, 1993)

Feist, *Luftwaffe in World War II: Part 3*, (Aero Pictorials series, No. 6; Aero, 1980)

Griehl, *Nightfighters over the Reich*, (Luftwaffe at War series, No. 2; Greenhill, London, 1997)

Gunston, B., *The Illustrated Encyclopedia of Combat Aircraft of World War II*, (Bookthrift, 1978)

Held and Nauroth, *Die deutsche Nachtjagd*, (Bildreport Weltkrieg II series (Motorbuch Verlag)

Hinchliffe, *Schnauffer: Ace of Diamonds*, (Tempus, Stroud, 1999)

Hopp, *Bf 110 G*, (Monogram Close-Up series, No. 18; Monogram Aviation Publications, 1986)

Jarrett, T. (ed.), *Aircraft of the Second World War: The Development of the Warplane 1939–49*, (Putnam's History of Aircraft series; Putnam, London, 1997)

Kit and Aders, *Chasseurs de Nuit Allemands de la Derniere Guerre*, (Editions Atlas, 1979)

Ledwoch, *Messerschmitt Bf 110*, (Aircraft Monograph series, No. 3; AJ Press, 1994)

Ledwoch, *Bf 110, vol. 2*, (Wydawnictwo Militaria series, No. 114; Wydawnictwo "Militaria", 2000)

Mackay, *Messerschmitt Bf 110*, (Crowood Aviation series; Crowood, 2000)

MacKay, *Messerschmitt Bf 110 G*, (Walk Around series, No. 24; Squadron/Signal, 2000)

Mankau and Petrick, *Messerschmitt Bf 110 – Me 210 – Me 410*, (Aviatic Verlag, 2001)

Merrick, *German Aircraft Interiors 1935–1945: Vol. 1*, (German Aircraft Interiors series, No. 1; Monogram Aviation Publications , 1996)

Nohara, *Luftwaffen Warplane 1928–45*, (Illustrated Warplane History series, No. 7; Green Arrow, 2001)

Nohara and Tanaka, *Messerschmitt Bf 110*, (Aero Detail series, No. 21; Dai-Nippon Kaiga Co., Ltd., 1998)

Philpott, *Fighters Defending the Reich*, (World War 2 Photo Album series, No. 4; Patrick Stephens, 1978)

Price, *Messerschmitt Bf 110 Night Fighters*, (Aircraft Profile series, No. 207; Profile Publications, 1971)

Price, *Battle over the Reich*, (Scribner's, 1973)

Pritchard, *Messerschmitt*, (Putnam, 1975)

Pritchard, *The Radar War*, (Patrick Stephens, 1989)

Ragni, *German Fighters of World War II*, (Squadron/Signal, 1979)

Reynolds, *Camouflage & Markings: Luftwaffe 1939–1945*, (Argus Books, 1992)

Ries, *Deutsche Luftwaffe über der Schweitz*, (Verlag Dieter Hoffmann, 1978)

Scutts, J., *German Night Fighter Aces of World War 2*, (Aircraft of the Aces 20, Osprey Publishing, Oxford, 1998)

Sheflin et al, *Airfoil 5*, (Airfoil series, No. 5; Airfoil Publications, 1987)

Streetly, *Confound & Destroy: 100 Group and the Bomber Support Campaign*, (Jane's, 1978)

Van Ishoven, *Messerschmitt Bf 110 at War*, (At War series; Ian Allan, London, 1985)

Weal, J., *Messerschmitt Bf 110* Zerstörer *Aces of World War 2*, (Aircraft of the Aces 25, Osprey Publishing, Oxford, 1999)

Widfeldt, *The Luftwaffe in Sweden, 1939–1945*, (Monogram Aviation Publications, 1983)

Windrow, M., *The Messerschmitt Bf 110*, (Aircraft Profile series, No. 23; Profile Publications)

Wood and Gunston, B., *Hitler's Luftwaffe*, (Salamander, 1977)

—— *Bf 110* (Famous Airplanes of the World (1) series, No. 38; Bunrin-Do, 1973)

—— *Luftfahrt International: No. 4* (Luftfahrt International series, No. 4; Verlag Karl R. Pawlas, 1974)

—— *Luftwaffe Night Fighters*, (Model Art Special Issue series, No. 480; Model Art, 1996)

—— *Luftwaffe Warbirds Photo Album, Vol. 1*, (Luftwaffe Warbirds Photo Album series, No. 1; Delta Publishing, 1992)

—— *Messerschmitt Bf 110*, (Famous Airplanes of the World (2) series, No. 41; Bunrin-Do, 1993)

Websites

HyperScale http://www.hyperscale.com

- Scale model related website including several articles and galleries on the Revell 1/48 scale Bf 110G-2/4 kits.

Additional Model Websites with Bf 110 Content

- Aircraft Resource Center http://www.aircraftresourcecenter.com
- Modeling Madness http://www.modelingmadness.com

IPMS Stockholm
   http://www.hotel.wineasy.se/ipms/stuff_eng_detail_bf110g.htm
Walkaround photographs of the Bf 110G-4 at the Royal Air Force Museum in Hendon

1/48-scale Messerschmitt Bf 110 decals

Brand	Description	Availability	Stock No.
AeroMaster	Bf 110 Stencils	Good	148021
AeroMaster	Messerschmitt Bf 110 Part II	Good	48331
AeroMaster	Nocturnal Birds of Prey Part I	Good	48559
AeroMaster	Nocturnal Birds of Prey Part II	Good	48567
Cutting Edge	Messerschmitt Bf 110G Pt 1	Good	CED48045
Cutting Edge	Messerschmitt Bf 110G Pt 2	Good	CED48046
EagleCals	Messerschmitt Bf 110C/E Night Fighters	Good	EC45
FCM	Battle of Britain. Includes Me 110C/D	Good	FCM4801
Hungarian	Messerschmitt Bf 110C/D	Out of Production	HAFD4813
Ministry of Small Aircraft Production	Me 110C/D/E (5) C 4N+ZL 3(F)22	Out of Production	MSAP7213
PD Models	Bf 110G Part 2	Good	PDD48007
PD Models	Bf 110G Part 1	Good	PDD48006
Revell/Monogram	Me-110 Decals	Good	81016
Superscale	Bf 110C Zerstorers	Good	480767
Superscale	Bf 110C Zerstorers	Good	480768
Tauro	Italian Squadron Insignia & Code	Good	48525
Techmod	Messerschmitt Bf-110C	Good	48011
Techmod	Messerschmitt Bf 110D	Good	48026
Techmod	Messerschmitt Bf 110C	Good	48049

1/48-scale Messerschmitt Bf 110 accessories

Brand	Description	Availability	Stock No.
Aires	Messerschmitt Bf 110G super detail set	Good	4891
Aires	Messerschmitt Bf 110G cockpit	Good	4857
Aires	DB605 engine	Good	4036
Aires	Messerschmitt Bf 110G-4 gun bay	Good	4880
Arba	Bf 110G-4 conversion for Fujimi	Out of Production	
Cutting Edge	Messerschmitt Bf 110G-4 open gun bay	Good	CEC48122
Cutting Edge	FuG 220 Lichtenstein SN-2b radar array	Good	CEC48200
Cutting Edge	FuG 220 Lichtenstein SN-2c radar array	Good	CEC48201
Cutting Edge	FuG 212 Lichtenstein C-1 thin post radar array	Good	CEC48203
Cutting Edge	FuG 212 Lichtenstein C-1 thick post radar array	Good	CEC48204
Cutting Edge	FuG 212 Lichtenstein C-1 conical radar array	Good	CEC48205
Cutting Edge	FuG 218 Neptun Radar for Messe	Good	CEC48206
Cutting Edge	FuG 227 Flensburg Radar	Good	CEC48207
Cutting Edge	FuG 220 Lichtenstein BC Radar	Good	CEC48208
Cutting Edge	Separate control surfaces	Good	CEC48245
Cutting Edge	Bf 110F/G Correction Set	Good	CEC48416
Czech Master Kits	Messerschmitt Bf 110G-2/R-1 conversion	Good	CMK4079
Eduard	Bf 110G detail set (brass etched)	Good	48192
Eduard	Bf 110C/D detail set (brass etched)	Good	48253
Eduard	Bf 110G Express Mask	Good	XF038
High Flight	Separate flaps	Out of Production	
Hi-Tech	BF 110G super detail set	Good	9012
Paragon Designs	Messerschmitt Bf 110C/G Open gun bay	Out of Production	48045
Squadron	Bf 110C/D Vacuform Canopy	Good	
Squadron	Bf 110 Vacuform Canopy	Good	SQ9566
Squadron	Bf 110G-4 Vacuform Canopy	Good	SQ9589
Tauro	DB 601 Engine	Good	TU48901
Tauro	DB 605 Engine	Good	TU48903
True Details	Bf 110G-4 Fast Frame	Good	TD41013
True Details	Bf 110C/D Zerstorer Fast Frame	Good	TD41021
True Details	Bf 110E/F/G Wheels	Good	TD48046
True Details	Bf 110C/D Wheels	Good	TD48077
True Details	Bf 110E/F/G Wheel Hub Mask	Good	TD83146
True Details	Bf 110C/D Wheel Hub Mask	Good	TD83177
True Details	Bf 110C/D Cockpit (resin)	Out of Production	
Verlinden Productions	Messerschmitt Bf 110G-4 update	Good	1252
Black Magic	Bf 110C/D Wheel Hub Masks for TD48077	Good	CEBM48033
Black Magic	Bf 110E/F/G Wheel Hub Masks for TD48046	Good	CEBM48034
Black Magic	Bf 110G Canopy & Wheel Hub Masks for ProModeler	Good	CEBM48035
Black Magic	Bf 110 70/71 Camouflage Masks	Good	CEBM48295
Black Magic	Bf 110 71/02 Camouflage Masks	Good	CEBM48296
Black Magic	Bf 110 74/75 Camouflage Masks	Good	CEBM48297
Black Magic	Bf 110C/D Canopy & Wheel Hub Masks for Fujimi	Good	CEBM48446
Moskit	Bf 110 exhausts for all day versions (hollow metal exhausts, 1/48)	Good	MOSK48003
Professional Model	Me 110G-2 w/3,7cm BK cannon & 4x WGr.21	Limited	PM48011

Index

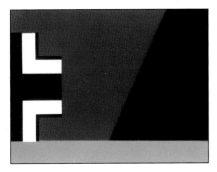

1.

2.

3.

4.

5.

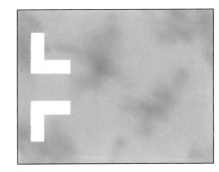

6.

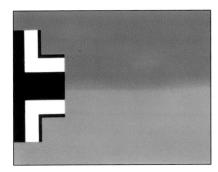

7.

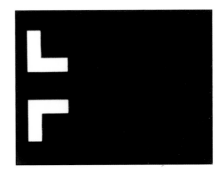

8.

Luftwaffe camouflage schemes were changed according to the widely varying theatres of action, and also in reaction to military developments. As one of the few aircraft that saw service from the first day of World War II to the last, the Messerschmitt Bf 110 wore a large selection of different Luftwaffe colours.

5.

Some pathfinder and special duties Bf 110s wore a scheme of overall RLM 76 Light Blue.

1.

The early war scheme of RLM 71 Dark Green, RLM 70 Black Green and RLM 65 Light Blue suited the dense forests of central Europe. It was also appropriate for a new air service unsure of its opponents' capabilities and response. The dark greens offered a measure of protection on the ground, under the canopy of trees, if fortunes turned against the Luftwaffe during its early campaigns.

6.

Early night fighters were painted black with an eggshell finish. This practice persisted until the introduction of the Bf 110G.

2.

Fortunes did not turn against the Luftwaffe. By 1940, the Messerschmitt Bf 110 had tasted success and was operating in more open countryside. During the invasion of the Low Countries and France, the Bf 110 was 'lightened up'. The RLM 70 Black Green was replaced with RLM 02 Grey (actually a green-grey shade). The fuselage demarcation line was frequently raised higher too, with a light mottle on the side of the aircraft. Many Bf 110s operating during the Battle of Britain also wore this scheme, but some retained their darker RLM 70/71 finish.

7.

The classic night fighter finish for the Messerschmitt Bf 110G-4 was a mottle of RLM 75 Grey Violet over an overall coat of RLM 76 Light Blue. In fact, it appears likely that many Bf 110G-4s were delivered in the day fighter scheme of RLM 74 and RLM 75 upper surfaces, and that the darker colours were partially oversprayed in the field to give the appearance of a grey mottle.

3.

In November 1941 the official Luftwaffe day-fighter camouflage scheme was changed to RLM 74 Grey Green, RLM 75 Grey Violet and RLM 76 Light Blue on the lower surfaces. Some Luftwaffe fighters had been painted in field-mixed greys for some time by the time the new orders were issued. Once again, it was common to see high demarcation lines and mottling on the fuselage.

8.

The final Messerschmitt Bf 110G-4s were delivered in a simple scheme of RLM 76 Light Blue lower surfaces and RLM 75 Grey Violet upper surfaces. The fuselage demarcation was usually high.

4.

Some Bf 110s operating in the Mediterranean were finished in the tropical colours of RLM 78 Sand Yellow and RLM 78 Blue. This paint was often applied with a very soft demarcation line along the centre of the fuselage.

Related titles & companion series from Osprey

For details of other available Osprey series go to
www.ospreypublishing.com or contact us – *see below*

To order any of these titles, or for more information on Osprey Publishing, contact:

Osprey Direct (UK) *Tel:* +44 (0)1933 443863 *Fax:* +44 (0)1933 443849 *E-mail:* info@ospreydirect.co.uk

Osprey Direct (USA) c/o MBI Publishing *Toll-free:* 1 800 826 6600 *Phone:* 1 715 294 3345
Fax: 1 715 294 4448 *E-mail:* info@ospreydirectusa.com

www.ospreypublishing.com

Expert advice on how to get the most from your modelling.

Modelling the Messerschmitt Bf 110

The Messerschmitt Bf 110 was undoubtedly one of the most significant aircraft of World War II. Despite suffering setbacks in the summer of 1940 at the hands of the RAF, it continued to be used effectively in other theatres and roles until the last days of the war, particularly as a night fighter against RAF Bomber Command strategic bombing campaign over the Reich. This title shows you how to correct and convert basic 1/48-scale kits of the Bf 110 into many different variants, using a wide selection of aftermarket detail sets, conversions, accessories and decals for both day and night fighter schemes.

Useful tips and techniques

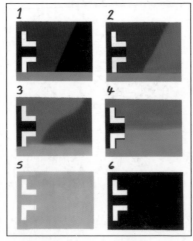

Full colour reference

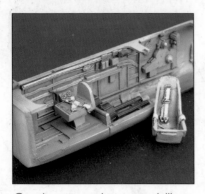

Creative approaches to modelling

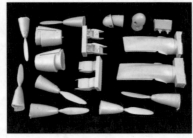

Step by step instructions

OSPREY
PUBLISHING

www.ospreypublishing.com

ISBN 1-84176-704-2

9 781841 767048

Napoleon's Balkan Troops

Vladimir Brnardic • Illustrated by Darko Pavlovic

VLADIMIR BRNARDIC was born in Zagreb in 1973. After graduating from the University of Zagreb with a History degree, he trained as a journalist. He has a keen interest in the history of Central and Eastern European military organisations, especially during the Napoleonic period. Vladimir is married and currently lives and works in Zagreb, Croatia.

DARKO PAVLOVIC was born in 1959 and currently lives and works in Zagreb, Croatia. A trained architect, he now works as a full-time illustrator and writer, specialising in militaria. Darko has illustrated a number of books for Osprey and has also written and illustrated titles for the Men-at-Arms series on the Austrian army of the 19th century.

CONTENTS